Regionalism and Supranationalism

Challenges and Alternatives to the Nation-State in Canada and Europe

Edited by
David M. Cameron

The Institute for Research on Public Policy
L'Institut de recherches politiques
and
Policy Studies Institute

© The Institute for Research on Public Policy and Policy Studies Institute 1981
All rights reserved
Printed in Canada

ISBN 0 920380 74 3

Legal Deposit First Quarter
Bibliothèque nationale du Québec

The Institute for Research on Public Policy/L'Institut de recherches politiques
2149 Mackay Street
Montreal, Quebec
H3G 2J2

Policy Studies Institute
1/2 Castle Lane
London SW1E 6DR

Founded in 1972, THE INSTITUTE FOR RESEARCH ON PUBLIC POLICY is a national organization whose independence and autonomy are ensured by the revenues of an endowment fund, which is supported by the federal and provincial governments and by the private sector. In addition, the Institute receives grants and contracts from governments, corporations, and foundations to carry out specific research projects.

The *raison d'être* of the Institute is threefold:

— To act as a catalyst within the national community by helping to facilitate informed public debate on issues of major public interest

— To stimulate participation by all segments of the national community in the process that leads to public policy making

— To find practical solutions to important public policy problems, thus aiding in the development of sound public policies

The Institute is governed by a Board of Directors, which is the decision-making body, and a Council of Trustees, which advises the board on matters related to the research direction of the Institute. Day-to-day administration of the Institute's policies, programmes, and staff is the responsibility of the president.

The Institute operates in a decentralized way, employing researchers located across Canada. This ensures that research undertaken will include contributions from all regions of the country.

Wherever possible, the Institute will try to promote public understanding of, and discussion on, issues of national importance, whether they be controversial or not. It will publish its research findings with clarity and impartiality. Conclusions or recommendations in the Institute's publications are solely those of the author, and should not be attributed to the Board of Directors, Council of Trustees, or contributors to the Institute.

The president bears final responsibility for the decision to publish a manuscript under the Institute's imprint. In reaching this decision, he is advised on the accuracy and objectivity of a manuscript by both Institute staff and outside reviewers. Publication of a manuscript signifies that it is deemed to be a competent treatment of a subject worthy of public consideration.

Publications of the Institute are published in the language of the author, along with an executive summary in both of Canada's official languages.

Institute Management

Foreword

In recent years it has become clear that the authority of the state has come under challenge from a variety of directions. Both in Canada and in the states of Western Europe, as well as in other parts of the world, the power of national governments has been subject to pressures both from within their own territory—demands for greater autonomy at regional levels—and from a number of powerful forces outside their frontiers. This relatively new phenomenon led to a decision by The Institute for Research on Public Policy and the European Centre for Political Studies (part of the Policy Studies Institute) to plan a joint study in order to make a systematic comparison of the impact of these new forces on Canada and on the states of Western Europe.

The various facets of the topic were explored in an intensive two-day seminar at the Policy Studies Institute in March 1980, on the basis of three papers by Canadian authors and three by Europeans: both the authors of papers and participants in the seminar included people with considerable practical experience of politics, as well as academic authorities. The seminar was generously supported by a grant from the Nuffield Foundation. The revised papers, published in this small volume together with some brief reflections on the seminar discussions, bring out a number of important considerations for policy makers both in Canada and in Europe: the study indicates a number of points of convergence between Canadian and European experience, as well as some contrasts, and it will make readers more aware of the reasons why national governments now have to operate in a new situation.

Roger Morgan
Head
European Centre for Political Studies
Policy Studies Institute
December 1980

Gordon Robertson
President
The Institute
for Research on Public Policy
December 1980

Avant-propos

Il est devenu évident, ces dernières années, que l'on conteste de toutes parts l'autorité de l'État. Tant au Canada qu'en Europe de l'Ouest et ailleurs au monde, le pouvoir des gouvernements nationaux est soumis à des pressions internes—des revendications en faveur d'une plus grande autonomie à l'échelon régional—et externes, en provenance de puissantes forces étrangères. Ce phénomène relativement récent a incité l'Institut de recherches politiques et le European Centre for Political Studies (faisant partie du Policy Studies Institute) à préparer une étude conjointe afin d'établir une comparaison systématique de l'incidence de ces nouvelles forces sur le Canada et sur les États de l'Europe occidentale.

On a pu, lors d'un colloque intensif de deux jours tenu en mars 1980 au Policy Studies Institute, se pencher sur les différents aspects de la question en s'inspirant de trois textes d'auteurs canadiens et de trois textes d'auteurs européens : on comptait, parmi les auteurs des textes et les participants au séminaire, des personnes ayant une expérience pratique considérable de la politique ainsi que des universitaires de renom. La Fondation Nuffield a accordé un appui généreux au colloque. Les textes remaniés et publiés dans ce petit ouvrage en compagnie de courtes réflexions sur les discussions engagées lors du colloque soulèvent un certain nombre de points importants qui méritent l'attention des décisionnaires tant européens que canadiens : l'étude fait voir certaines similitudes et différences entre l'expérience canadienne et européenne tout en éveillant le lecteur aux raisons pour lesquelles les gouvernements doivent maintenant opérer dans une nouvelle situation.

Roger Morgan
Directeur
European Centre for Political Studies
Policy Studies Institute
Décembre 1980

Gordon Robertson
Président
L'Institut
de recherches politiques
Décembre 1980

Table of Contents

The Authors

Raymond Breton is Professor of Sociology in the University of Toronto and Director of the Ethnic and Cultural Diversity Programme of the Institute for Research on Public Policy, Toronto, Canada.

David M. Cameron is Professor and Director of the School of Public Administration in Dalhousie University, Halifax, Canada.

Gordon Smith is Senior Lecturer in Government in the London School of Economics and Political Science, London, England.

Denis Stairs is Professor of Political Science in Dalhousie University, Halifax, Canada.

Jacques Vandamme is Professor of Law in the Catholic University of Louvain, Brussels, Belgium.

Helen Wallace is Lecturer in Public Administration in the Civil Service College, London, England, and in 1979-80 was seconded to the Planning Staff, Foreign and Commonwealth Office, Government of the United Kingdom.

Ronald L. Watts is Principal of Queen's University, Kingston, Canada.

Introduction and Summary

The time is right for a serious examination of regionalism and supranationalism in Canada and Europe. On both sides of the Atlantic, political events and pressures are forcing a re-evaluation of existing political structures with a view not merely to their adequacy but increasingly to the likelihood of their survival. The more visible events and pressures are obvious enough, from a Quebec referendum on sovereignty-association on the one hand, to the direct election of a European Parliament on the other. What is obvious, then, is that contemporary political events are characterized by forces pushing simultaneously in two opposite directions: toward smaller, or at least more decentralized, structures, and simultaneously toward larger, more integrative systems. The first of these is captured by the notion of regionalism and the second by supranationalism.

The appropriateness of a comparative study of Canada and Europe arises from both the similarities and differences of the two areas. Both share traditions and values of constitutional and representative government, both are part of a Western industrial economic system, both are continental in territorial scope, both are allied to but somewhat apprehensive about the United States as super-power. Conversely, Europe comprises autonomous nation-states separated by history, custom, and language, and joined in a relatively new and fragile economic and political community, while Canada is a federation of over a century's standing whose provinces act increasingly like nation-states. It is in this latter context that comparisons become especially inviting. Is it possible to shed light upon the nature of regionalism and continental integration in Canada and Europe by examining the experience of the other? That the answer to this question would be positive constituted one of the two principal impulses behind the organization of the seminar on federalism, regionalism, and supranationalism by the Institute for Research on Public Policy/Policy Studies Institute in the spring of 1980. The second impulse was collectively to focus the minds of a group of senior Canadian and European scholars upon the meaning and implications of regionalism and supranationalism *per se*. Thus the objective of the seminar, and consequently of this book, was to increase our knowledge of regionalism and supranationalism as political phenomena, and to explore similarities and differences in the manifestation of these phenomena in Europe and in Canada.

This dual objective accounts for the topics selected for papers and the organization of this book. Three papers were invited from Canadian and European authors respectively. The first set would provide a review or overview of factors underlying the phenomena of regionalism and supranationalism generally, not necessarily within Canada or Europe, but from a

Canadian or European perspective. The second pair of papers would then examine regionalism both within and from the perspective of Europe and Canada. Finally, a third set of papers would explore supranational integration within the context of its nature and meaning for Canada and Europe.

This book is similarly organized. Part One constitutes an examination of ideas, forces, and perspectives that provide a framework or context for regionalism and supranationalism. Here, the very selection of the two chapter titles anticipates what will become a theme of the entire project: Canadians and Europeans approach questions of regionalism and supranationalism from quite different perspectives. Professor Watts' initial Canadian paper, constituting Chapter One, accurately reflects the Canadian perspective by centring its inquiry upon the concept and scope of federalism. Dr. Gordon Smith similarly reflects the European perspective in organizing Chapter Two around the idea of the nation-state. Again and again throughout the seminar and throughout this book, the significance of these different starting points is underscored. To an amazing extent, regionalism and supranationalism are approached from the perspective of a federation in Canada and of nation-states in Europe. Beyond this anticipation of discussions to come, the two chapters in Part One together represent a most effective treatment of the central concerns of the seminar and the book.

Ronald Watts begins Chapter One by observing that modern society is characterized by "pressures not only for larger states but also for smaller ones." Pressures toward economic, social, and political integration are examined, as are pressures toward regionalism, which Professor Watts suggests are essentially reactions against the size and distance that characterize the large, technocratic state. Regionalism will be particularly strong where these universal phenomena are supported by historical, cultural, and especially linguistic distinctiveness. Professor Watts then examines the idea of federalism as one device potentially capable of containing, if not reconciling, these contradictory pressures. Federalism is born of a balance between integrative and disintegrative pressures, however, and cannot itself effect such a balance. Where pressures for either integration or regionalism overwhelm the other, federalism cannot survive. Federalism is thus one of several organizational forms that occupy the spectrum from political integration to disintegration. But while federalism as an idea has a number of necessary properties, which Professor Watts reviews, no two federations will be exactly alike, for each must adapt and be adapted to the peculiar situation in which it is to take root. Federalism remains an idea uniquely capable of responding to simultaneous pressures toward integration and disintegration.

Gordon Smith draws remarkably similar conclusions, although he starts from a very different perspective. Concerned as to whether the multiple pressures on the contemporary West European state can be related in a coherent way, he poses and examines three attributes of the successful state. The state serves as guarantor of territorial integrity and economic autonomy, it is shaped by an appropriate boundary between itself and society, and it enjoys a legitimacy derived from popular support. The contemporary West European states have long since lost the capacity independently to guarantee integrity or autonomy, while the state-society line has become so blurred that the state is in danger of being overwhelmed by societal demands. Popular support or loyalty must be earned by appropriate performance, and it is precisely the inability of the nation-state to offer such performance that leads to a shift in the locus of popular support. Such a shift could operate in the direction of supranationalism, but the European Community is even less capable of earning support than the nation-state. The alternative, of course, is regionalism and the shift of loyalties to sub-national units. This phenomenon might be resisted, through attempts to strengthen or democratize the nation-state, or it might be accepted in fostering the decentralization of the state. Dr. Smith thus offers federalism as a possible and desirable solution to the problems of the European nation-state. He reviews European experience with federalism—shaped by cultural and linguistic differences as in Switzerland and now in Spain and perhaps Belgium, and deliberately adopted as a matter of constitutional policy as in West Germany and Italy. Dr. Smith and Professor Watts thus both endorse federalism as an appropriate response to pressures for integration and disintegration. But for Dr. Smith, federalism in Europe is seen as appropriate to the task of decentralizing political authority *below* the level of the nation-state rather than of collapsing nation-states into a continental federation. In this perspective, supranationalism gives way to regionalism.

As indicated earlier, Part Two contains two chapters respectively examining regionalism in Europe and Canada. Together, these chapters not only add considerably to our understanding of the concept of regionalism, but also reveal significant differences both in the perspectives of European and Canadian scholarship and in the experiences with regionalism in Europe and Canada.

Jacques Vandamme approaches the topic of European regionalism from a perspective similar to that of Gordon Smith. Supranationalism, he suggests, is a contemporary response to economic and technological necessity. Regionalism, on the other hand, must be seen as resulting from two quite distinct impulses. First, regionalism may be the result of deliberate central policy—described as functional *regionalization*—whose concern is with decentralized administration and physical planning. Second, regionalism may also emerge in the form of local autonomy, the desire of a self-conscious community to acquire a degree of political independence. The two phenomena are very usefully distinguished as regionalization on the one hand, and regionalism on the other.

Professor Vandamme considers the cases of West Germany, Italy, and Belgium as offering a variety of instances of regionalism and regional policy. West Germany was deliberately regionalized following the Second World

War, but its regionalization took the form of federalism, and at least partly because of that, West Germany has successfully contained and responded to subsequent regional pressures. Italy established the framework for regionalism in 1948, but adopted an active policy of regionalization only in 1970, a policy largely aimed at stabilizing the central state. Belgium, of course, has the most complex experience, and Professor Vandamme very effectively describes recent attempts to combine regionalization with an accommodation of regionalism in what may ultimately yield a modified and asymmetrical form of federalism.

Professor Vandamme's conclusions—that the lack of success of the nation-state in coping with contemporary economic problems is behind both regionalism and regionalization—support the arguments developed earlier by Gordon Smith. Neither regionalization, regionalism, nor supranationalism hold the key to the future of Europe. On the contrary, each can be understood only in relation to what remains Europe's primary political structure: the autonomous nation-state.

Raymond Breton begins his examination of Canadian regionalism with a most useful definition. Regionalism, he suggests, is a socio-psychological phenomenon that refers to a territorial space, its people, and its institutions. It is also a political phenomenon in so far as economic, political, and cultural *interests* are defined and articulated in regional terms. A region is an *institutional system*; a regionalized country is one composed of territorially defined institutional sub-systems within which people actually carry on the business of living.

According to Professor Breton, regions are measured by the institutional discontinuities that mark them off from each other. These discontinuities may be limited or extensive (at the latter extreme, regionalism slips over into nationalism). The fact that, in Canada, regions and provinces now unquestionably coincide gives to Canadian regionalism at once its unique character and its most powerful characteristic.

Professor Breton offers a further useful distinction: between protest and entrepreneurial regionalism. The former seeks to protect regional institutions from external pressures (including those emanating from the central government and "masked" as national policies); the latter represents an attempt to give fuller expression to the institutional ambitions peculiar to a specific region. The two make common cause in opposing the aggrandizement of the central order of government and seek instead to strengthen provincial authority.

In Part Three, discussion shifts from regionalism to supranationalism. Here, Canadian and European differences become most apparent. The central issue posed by supranational integration in Europe is nicely captured by the phrase "creeping federalism." In Canada, federalism is not even discussed in the context of supranationalism. Rather, the debate centres upon a quite different concept: American penetration of Canadian institutions.

The theme of American penetration is discussed in a remarkable chapter prepared by Denis Stairs. Here, the cacophony of voices arguing at cross purposes over the extent, meaning, and consequences of American influences on Canada are organized into five schools of protest. Each school (or focus of anxiety) is primarily concerned with one form or arena of interaction, and each accepts the logical opposite as more desirable. No school, and virtually no Canadian protagonist, accepts continental integration—implying some form of union with the United States—as an acceptable objective of public policy. The five schools of protest that Professor Stairs reviews with a great deal of understanding and no small amount of humour are those originating respectively from a bureaucratic, economic, cultural, informational, and philosophical perspective.

Professor Stairs notes that those who denounce integration seldom have a concrete image of that which they so strongly oppose—no image, that is, of what an integrated continent would look like. On both sides, therefore, the arguments remain disaggregated. So it is with policy responses to the "problem" of continental pressure. Not only is there no agreement on the nature of the problem, but both it and proposed solutions invariably generate different kinds and degrees of support or opposition among Canada's regions and their provincial governments. Professor Stairs examines five strategies open to the Canadian federal government: diversification, multilateraliza-tion, fragmentation, substitution (or nation building), and disengagement. He concludes that each of these strategies—and not the success or defeat of any of them—is likely to continue to occupy a place in the structure of Canadian policy responses to American penetration.

Helen Wallace's Chapter Six demonstrates how different is the European experience with continental integration. For Europe, of course, all questions of integration centre on the European Community (EC), yet even here experience is ambivalent. Early assumptions of impending political union have given way to sceptical analyses, yet the Community expands in size and its institutions acquire deeper roots. Confirming the centrality of the nation-state, Dr. Wallace argues that analysis of the EC requires a careful analysis of its impact on its component parts. She then poses and considers three questions: is the impact of the EC on its members different in kind from that of other forms of international co-operation; what is the nature of the EC's impact on the politics of its members; what are the factors that determine the way in which member states respond to the EC?

The answer to the first question is positive, but also complex. As Dr. Wallace notes, "the Community is . . . a special form of international co-operation precisely because its common legislation has direct policy effects on the member states and because it offers the opportunity for the pursuit of specific interests through collective action." Similarly, the second question yields a complex answer, for the obvious and material benefits of the Community have given way to highly politicized interstate and inter-interest bargaining. Discussion of the third question leads to a revealing consideration of factors that incline member states to support or oppose further integration. As European policies have come to depend upon the consent of national publics, the dependence of the EC upon member states to shape, if not to "deliver," popular support becomes more critical. The directly elected Parliament becomes especially important in so far as it will succeed or fail in modifying this relationship. Direct contact between citizen and Community, and the sense of a European political community that might thus be engendered, remains the measure of the distance between the EC and a true federation. Dr. Wallace is doubtful that this situation will change dramatically in the foreseeable future; more likely is a continued strengthening of Community policies and institutions, coupled simultaneously with national opposition to extensions of the Community's penetration into the nation-state.

> Community government co-exists with national government but cannot be separated from it. It remains dependent on what politics within individual member states will permit.

If nothing else, the chapters of this book reveal profound similarities and differences in the approaches of Canadians and Europeans to questions of regionalism and supranationalism. The book concludes with some comments by the editor that seek to define, describe, and organize these, drawing upon the seminar discussions for much of the material and ideas. This does not, however, seek to represent a fair reproduction of the conversations and arguments that actually took place. Rather, with editorial if not artistic licence, it seeks merely to identify and integrate some of the threads that ran through those discussions. The ultimate conclusion is a simple but important one: while Canadians and Europeans have much to learn from each other, and while there is considerable similarity in their respective understandings of regionalism, federalism, and supranationalism, the reality of institutional evolution and experience is such that no generalized lessons can be drawn for the future. Regionalism, federalism, and supranationalism can indeed be usefully studied from a comparative perspective, but while the results of such study shed light on the respective settings, they offer little support for the formulation of grand theories of political change or development. Since that is a conclusion the thoughtful person might well have reached without the benefit of this book, it should not detract from the more demanding, but more rewarding, task of seeking to understand the very important phenomena of contemporary regionalism and supranationalism in Europe and Canada. For that, the reader is invited to make use of the six excellent chapters that constitute the substance of this book.

Introduction et abrégé

Le moment est propice à un examen sérieux du régionalisme et du supranationalisme au Canada et en Europe. Des deux côtés de l'Atlantique, la conjoncture et les pressions politiques nous obligent à réévaluer les structures politiques existantes non seulement du point de vue de leur pertinence mais d'une manière croissante quant à la probabilité de leur survie. Certains événements et pressions sont assez évidents, du référendum sur la souveraineté-association au Québec d'une part à l'élection directe du Parlement européen d'autre part. Ce qui est évident, donc, c'est que les événements politiques contemporains sont caractérisés par un jeu de forces opposées qui poussent à la fois vers des structures plus petites, ou du moins plus décentralisées, et vers des systèmes plus gros, plus intégrants. La première de ces réalités est cernée par le concept de régionalisme, et la deuxième, par celui de supranationalisme.

L'à-propos d'une étude comparative du Canada et de l'Europe ressort à la fois des ressemblances et des différences entre les deux zones. Elles partagent toutes deux les traditions et les valeurs que représente un gouvernement constitutionnel et représentatif; les deux font partie d'un système économique industriel occidental; les deux ont un territoire à caractère continental; et les deux sont alliées des États-Unis, bien que le statut de superpuissance de ce dernier leur cause quelque appréhension. Par contre, l'Europe se compose d'États-nations autonomes, distincts par l'histoire, les coutumes et les langues, mais réunis dans une communauté économique et politique relativement nouvelle et fragile, tandis que le Canada est une fédération qui dure depuis plus de cent ans, dont les provinces se comportent de plus en plus en États-nations. Les comparaisons sont particulièrement attrayantes dans ce dernier contexte. Est-il possible d'éclairer la nature du régionalisme et de l'intégration continentale au Canada et en Europe en examinant l'expérience de l'autre? L'espoir d'une réponse affirmative constitua l'une des deux principales impulsions derrière la mise sur pied du séminaire organisé au printemps 1980 par l'Institut des études politiques et l'Institut de recherches politiques. Le désir de provoquer la réflexion d'un groupe d'universitaires chevronnés du Canada et de l'Europe sur la signification et les répercussions du régionalisme et du supranationalisme *en soi* constitua la deuxième impulsion. Ainsi, l'objectif du séminaire, et par conséquent de ce livre, était d'augmenter nos connaissances du régionalisme et du supranationalisme en tant que phénomènes politiques, et d'explorer les similitudes et les différences lors de la manifestation de ces phénomènes en Europe et au Canada.

Ce double objectif explique les thèmes choisis pour les communications ainsi que l'organisation de ce livre. On sollicita trois communications d'auteurs canadiens et trois d'auteurs européens. Le premier ensemble présenterait un examen ou un survol des facteurs sous-jacents du régionalisme et du supranationalisme en général, pas nécessairement au Canada ou en Europe mais d'un point de vue européen ou canadien. La deuxième paire de documents examinerait ensuite le régionalisme à la fois de l'intérieur, et de l'Europe et du Canada. Enfin, un troisième ensemble de documents explorerait l'intégration supranationale tant dans sa nature que dans sa signification pour le Canada et l'Europe.

Ce livre est organisé de semblable manière. La première partie fait l'examen des idées, des forces et des points de vue qui fournissent un cadre ou un contexte au régionalisme et au supranationalisme. Ici, le choix même des deux titres de chapitre présage ce qui deviendra un thème du projet tout entier : Canadiens et Européens abordent les questions de régionalisme et de supranationalisme de points de vue très différents. Le premier texte canadien, du professeur Watts, qui forme le chapitre un, reflète fidèlement le point de vue canadien en centrant l'enquête sur le concept et la portée du fédéralisme. Le professeur Smith reflète à son tour le point de vue européen en organisant le chapitre deux autour de l'idée de l'État-nation. L'importance de ces points de départ différents est soulignée à maintes reprises tout au long du séminaire et de ce livre. Il est étonnant de voir à quel point le régionalisme et le supranationalisme sont abordés du point de vue d'une fédération au Canada et d'États-nations en Europe. Au-delà de cette anticipation des discussions à venir, les deux chapitres de la première partie représentent une manière fort valable de traiter les principaux sujets du séminaire et du livre.

Ronald Watts commence le premier chapitre en observant que la société moderne est caractérisée par des '' pressions non seulement en faveur d'États plus grands, mais aussi de plus petits ''. On y examine les pressions en faveur de l'intégration économique, sociale et politique de même que celles en faveur du régionalisme, qui sont, selon le professeur Watts, essentielle- ment des réactions contre la taille et l'éloignement qui caractérisent le grand État technocratique. Le régionalisme sera particulièrement fort là où des différences historiques, culturelles et, surtout, linguistiques viennent ren- forcer ces phénomènes. Le professeur Watts examine ensuite le concept du fédéralisme en tant que mécanisme susceptible de contenir, sinon réconcilier ces pressions opposées. Le fédéralisme naît d'un équilibre entre des pressions d'intégration et de fractionnement, mais il ne peut de lui-même réaliser un tel équilibre. Le fédéralisme ne peut survivre là où des pressions soit vers le régionalisme, soit vers l'intégration écrasent la tendance opposée. Il est donc une des formes d'organisation dans la gamme qui va de l'intégration au fractionnement politique. Mais, bien que le concept du fédéralisme ait certains des attributs nécessaires, que le professeur Watts examine, il n'y aura pas deux fédérations identiques, car chacune doit s'adapter et être ajustée à la situation particulière dans laquelle elle doit s'enraciner. Le fédéralisme est un concept unique en son genre par sa capacité de répondre simultanément à des pressions vers l'intégration et vers le fractionnement.

Gordon Smith tire des conclusions remarquablement semblables, malgré son point de départ très différent. Préoccupé de voir si l'on peut établir des rapports cohérents entre les nombreuses pressions qui s'exercent sur l'État contemporain d'Europe occidentale, il énonce et étudie trois attributs de l'État réussi. L'État est le garant de l'intégrité territoriale et de l'autonomie économique; il a une forme déterminée par une frontière appropriée entre la société et lui-même; et il jouit d'une légitimité qu'il tire de l'appui populaire. Les États contemporains d'Europe occidentale ont depuis longtemps perdu la capacité de garantir indépendamment l'intégrité territoriale et l'autonomie économique, tandis que la démarcation société-État est devenue si embrouillée que l'État court le risque d'être débordé par les exigences de la société. L'appui populaire ou la loyauté doit se gagner par un rendement approprié, que l'État-nation ne peut justement pas donner, ce qui provoque un déplacement de cet appui. Un tel déplacement pourrait s'opérer en faveur du supranationalisme, mais la Communauté européenne est encore moins capable de s'attirer l'appui que l'État-nation. L'autre choix, bien sûr, est le régionalisme et le déplacement des loyautés vers des administrations infranationales. On pourrait résister à cette tendance en essayant de renforcer ou démocratiser l'État-nation, ou on pourrait l'accepter dans le but de favoriser la décentralisation de l'État. Le professeur Smith propose ainsi le fédéralisme comme une solution possible et désirable aux problèmes de l'État-nation européen. Il examine l'expérience européenne du fédéralisme, que ce soit une expérience façonnée par des différences linguistiques et culturelles comme en Suisse, en Espagne maintenant et peut-être en Belgique, ou volontairement adoptée comme politique constitutionnelle, en Allemagne de l'Ouest et en Italie notamment. Les professeurs Smith et Watts endossent ainsi tous deux le fédéralisme en tant que réaction appropriée à des pressions vers l'intégration et vers le fractionnement. Pour le professeur Smith, cependant, le fédéralisme en Europe convient à la décentralisation de l'autorité politique *sous* le niveau de l'État-nation plutôt qu'à l'affaissement des États-nations en une fédération continentale. Pour le professeur Smith, le supranationalisme cède la voie au régionalisme.

Comme on l'a indiqué plus tôt, la deuxième partie compte deux chapitres qui font l'examen du régionalisme en Europe et au Canada respectivement. Pris ensemble, ces deux chapitres ajoutent non seulement beaucoup à notre entendement du concept du régionalisme, mais révèlent également des différences importantes tant dans les points de vue des universitaires canadiens et européens que dans le vécu du régionalisme en Europe et au Canada.

Jacques Vandamme aborde le sujet du régionalisme européen d'un point de vue semblable à celui de Gordon Smith. Il laisse entendre que le supranationalisme est une réaction contemporaine à des besoins économiques et techniques. Le régionalisme, d'autre part, doit se voir comme résultant de deux impulsions très distinctes. Le régionalisme peut d'abord être le résultat d'une politique centrale délibérée—décrite comme une *régionalisation fonctionnelle*—qui se préoccupe d'administration décentralisée et de planification territoriale. Deuxièmement, le régionalisme peut aussi apparaître sous la forme d'autonomie locale, le désir d'une communauté consciente d'elle-même d'acquérir un degré d'indépendance politique. On distingue utilement les deux phénomènes en parlant de régionalisation d'une part et de régionalisme d'autre part.

Le professeur Vandamme examine les cas de l'Allemagne de l'Ouest, de l'Italie et de la Belgique comme exemples de régionalisme et de politique régionale. L'Allemagne de l'Ouest fut délibérément régionalisée après la Seconde Guerre mondiale, mais sa régionalisation prit la forme d'un fédéralisme, et c'est au moins en partie à cause de cela qu'elle a pu résister et réagir avec succès à des pressions régionales subséquentes. L'Italie établit le cadre d'un régionalisme en 1948, mais n'adopta une politique active de régionalisation qu'en 1970, une politique en grande partie dirigée vers la stabilisation de l'État central. La Belgique a bien sûr l'expérience la plus complexe, et le professeur Vandamme décrit fort bien des tentatives récentes de combiner la régionalisation avec un accommodement du régionalisme selon une formule qui pourrait, en fin de compte, produire une forme modifiée et asymétrique du fédéralisme.

Les conclusions du professeur Vandamme voulant que l'échec de l'État-nation face aux problèmes économiques contemporains provoque à la fois le régionalisme et la régionalisation étayent l'argumentation que Gordon Smith développait plus tôt. La régionalisation, non plus que le régionalisme ou le supranationalisme, n'est pas la clé de l'avenir de l'Europe. Au contraire, chacun d'eux ne se comprend seulement qu'en rapport avec ce qui demeure la principale structure politique de l'Europe : l'État-nation autonome.

Raymond Breton commence son examen du régionalisme canadien par une définition des plus utiles. Le régionalisme, propose-t-il, est un phénomène psychosocial qui renvoie à un espace territorial, à ses gens et à ses institutions. C'est également un phénomène politique dans la mesure où les *intérêts* économiques, politiques et culturels sont définis et articulés en termes régionaux. Une région est un *réseau d'institutions* : un pays régionalisé en est un composé de sous-réseaux d'institutions territorialement définis à l'intérieur desquels les gens s'occupent réellement de vivre leur vie.

Selon le professeur Breton, on mesure les régions aux disjonctions des institutions, qui les séparent les unes des autres. Ces disjonctions peuvent être limitées ou étendues (à ce dernier extrême, le régionalisme glisse vers le nationalisme). Le fait qu'au Canada, provinces et régions soient maintenant sans aucun doute synonymes donne au régionalisme canadien à la fois sa plus puissante caractéristique et son caractère unique.

Le professeur Breton offre une autre distinction utile entre le régionalisme de protestation et le régionalisme d'entreprise. Le premier cherche à protéger les institutions régionales contre les pressions externes (y compris celles qui émanent du gouvernement central sous le " voile " de l'intérêt national); le second représente une tentative d'exprimer plus complètement les désirs particuliers d'une région spécifique au sujet des institutions. Les deux font cause commune face à l'accroissement de l'ordre central de gouvernement et cherchent au contraire à renforcer le pouvoir provincial.

Dans la troisième partie, la discussion passe du régionalisme au supranationalisme. Les différences entre le Canada et l'Europe deviennent ici les plus évidentes. La problématique que pose pour l'Europe le supranationalisme est bien rendue par l'expression " fédéralisme envahissant ". Au Canada, l'on ne discute même pas du fédéralisme dans le contexte du supranationalisme. Les débats se circonscrivent plutôt autour d'un concept très différent : la pénétration américaine des institutions canadiennes.

Denis Stairs, dans un chapitre remarquable, aborde le thème de la pénétration américaine. Ici, la cacophonie des voix entretenant un dialogue de sourds au sujet de la portée, de la signification et des conséquences des influences américaines sur le Canada se répartit en cinq mouvements de protestation. Chaque mouvement (ou foyer d'angoisses) s'intéresse avant tout à une forme ou à un champ d'interaction, et chacun considère son opposé logique comme plus désirable. Aucun mouvement, et pratiquement aucun protagoniste canadien, n'accepte que l'intégration continentale, qui impliquerait une forme quelconque d'union avec les États-Unis, soit un objectif acceptable de la politique d'État. Les cinq mouvements de protestation, que le professeur Stairs examine avec beaucoup de compréhension et une large part d'humour, émanent respectivement de points de vue bureaucratique, économique, culturel, informationnel et philosophique.

Le professeur Stairs note que ceux qui dénoncent l'intégration ont rarement une image concrète de ce à quoi ils s'opposent si fortement—aucune image, c'est-à-dire, de ce qu'un continent intégré aurait l'air. Ainsi donc, les arguments restent éparpillés des deux côtés. Il en est de même quant à la réponse politique au " problème " de la pression vers le continentalisme. Non seulement n'y a-t-il pas d'accord sur la nature du problème, mais il ne manque pas, en compagnie des solutions proposées, de susciter divers types et divers degrés d'appui ou d'opposition dans les régions du Canada et chez leurs gouvernements provinciaux. Le professeur Stairs examine cinq stratégies dont le gouvernement fédéral canadien dispose : la diversification, la multilatéralisation, la fragmentation, la substitution (ou l'édification nationale) et le désengagement. Il conclut que chacune de ces stratégies (et non le succès ou l'échec de l'une d'elles) continuera probablement à occuper une place dans la structure de la réaction politique canadienne à la pénétration américaine.

Le chapitre 6, de Helen Wallace, démontre combien différente est l'expérience européenne de l'intégration continentale. Pour l'Europe, bien sûr, toutes les questions d'intégration se rapportent à la Communauté européenne (CE); cependant, l'expérience y est tout aussi ambivalente. Les présomptions de la première heure voulant que l'union politique soit imminente ont cédé la place à des analyses sceptiques, alors même que la Communauté s'élargit et que ses institutions s'enracinent plus profondément. Confirmant le rôle central de l'État-nation, le professeur Wallace fait valoir qu'une analyse de la CE requiert une analyse soignée de son effet sur ses parties composantes. Elle pose et considère ensuite trois questions : l'effet de la CE sur ses membres est-il de nature différente de l'effet produit par d'autres formes de coopération internationale; quelle est la nature de l'effet de la CE sur les politiques de ses membres; quels sont les facteurs qui déterminent la façon dont les États membres de la CE y réagissent?

La réponse à la première question est affirmative, mais complexe aussi. Comme le note le professeur Wallace, '' la Communauté est (...) une forme spéciale de coopération internationale justement parce que sa législation commune a des effets directs sur les politiques des États membres, et parce qu'elle offre la possibilité de poursuivre des intérêts précis au moyen d'une action collective ''. De la même manière, la deuxième question produit une réponse complexe, car les bienfaits évidents et les avantages matériels de la Communauté ont cédé le pas à une négociation hautement politisée entre États et entre intérêts. La discussion de la troisième question amène l'étude révélatrice des facteurs qui portent les États membres à appuyer une plus grande intégration ou à s'y opposer. La dépendance de la CE vis-à-vis ses États membres pour former sinon '' livrer '' l'appui populaire devient plus critique étant donné que les politiques européennes dépendent maintenant du consentement des publics nationaux. Le Parlement directement élu prend une importance particulière dans la mesure où c'est lui qui réussira ou échouera à la tâche de modifier cette relation. Le contact direct entre le citoyen et la Communauté, et le sens d'une communauté politique européenne qui pourrait s'ensuivre sont la mesure de l'éloignement entre la CE et une vraie fédération. Le professeur Wallace doute que cette situation se modifie radicalement dans un avenir prévisible; il est plus probable que les politiques et les institutions de la Communauté vont continuer de s'affermir, en même temps que se manifestera l'opposition nationale à de plus grandes pénétrations de la Communauté dans l'État-nation.

> Le gouvernement de la Communauté co-existe avec le gouvernement national mais ne peut en être séparé. Il dépend toujours de ce que permet la politique à l'intérieur de chacun des États membres.

Les chapitres de ce livre révèlent à tout le moins des ressemblances et des différences profondes dans la façon d'aborder les questions de régionalisme et de supranationalisme par les Canadiens et les Européens. Le livre s'achève sur des commentaires de l'éditeur, commentaires qui cherchent à définir, à décrire et à organiser ces questions en s'inspirant des discussions du séminaire. Ils ne prétendent pas, cependant, être une reproduction juste des conversations et des débats qui eurent véritablement lieu. Ils cherchent plutôt, avec la licence de l'éditeur sinon celle de l'artiste, simplement à identifier et réunir certains des fils conducteurs présents dans ces discussions. La dernière conclusion est simple mais d'importance : bien que les Canadiens et les Européens aient beaucoup à apprendre les uns des autres et qu'il y ait une ressemblance considérable dans leur entendement respectif du régionalisme, du fédéralisme et du supranationalisme, la réalité de la pratique et de l'évolution des institutions est telle qu'on n'en peut retirer aucune leçon de portée générale pour l'avenir. L'on peut certainement tirer profit d'une étude comparative du régionalisme, du fédéralisme et du supranationalisme; cependant, même si les résultats de telles études éclairent les contextes respectifs, ils offrent peu d'appui à la formulation de grandes théories de changement ou de développement politique. Puisque voilà une conclusion à laquelle une personne réfléchie aurait pu arriver sans l'avantage de ce livre, elle ne doit pas nuire à la tâche plus exigente, mais plus profitable, de chercher à comprendre les phénomènes très importants que sont le régionalisme et le supranationalisme contemporains en Europe et au Canada. Pour ce faire, on invite le lecteur à utiliser les six excellents chapitres qui constituent l'essentiel de ce livre.

Part One

Chapter One

Federalism, Regionalism, and Political Integration

by
Ronald L. Watts

Writing in 1939, Harold Laski, in an article entitled "The Obsolescence of Federalism," declared: "I infer in a word that the epoch of federalism is over."[1] Federal government in its traditional form, with its compartmenting of functions, rigidity, legalism, and conservatism was, he argued, incapable of coping with giant capitalism and the demands for large-scale government action. Even K.C. Wheare, much more sympathetic to the potentialities of federal government, conceded in the preface and conclusion to the first edition of his study, *Federal Government*, in 1945, that under the pressures of economic and international crises, the trend appeared to be toward a concentration of central powers incompatible with the federal principle. In contrast, the last thirty-five years have seen the proliferation of federal experiments in Europe, Africa, Asia, and South and North America, many of them multinational in composition.

Contrary to the earlier expectations, the experience of both developed and developing nation-states indicates that modern developments in transportation, social communications, technology, and industrial organization have produced pressures not only for larger states but also for smaller ones. Thus, as Clifford Geertz has pointed out, there have developed "two powerful, thoroughly interdependent, yet distinct and often actually opposed motives":[2] the desire to build an efficient and dynamic modern state, and the search for identity. The former is generated by the goals and values shared by most Western and non-Western societies today: a desire for progress, a rising standard of living, social justice and influence in the world arena; and by a growing awareness of world-wide interdependence in an era whose advanced technology makes both mass destruction and mass construction possible.[3] The latter arises from the desire for smaller, self-governing political units more responsive to the individual citizen and the desire to give expression to primary group attachments—religious connections, linguistic and cultural

3

ties, historical traditions, and social practices—which provide the distinctive basis for a community's sense of identity and yearning for self-determination.

The latter half of the twentieth century has seen these two forces in tension producing contradictory political trends in the direction of integration and disintegration. The same period, which saw the establishment of supranational associations and organizations such as the European Community, the Andrean Development Corporation, the East African Common Market, the Organization of American States, the North Atlantic Treaty Organisation, the Warsaw Pact, the Cominform, and the United Nations, also saw the establishment of so many small states that Ivo Duchachek has referred to the late 1960s as a period "not only of miniskirts but also of ministates."[4] The increasing number of microstates, states whose viability is often rightly in doubt, gives evidence of the strength of the desires, particularly in former colonial areas, to "go it alone." Furthermore, ferment over such issues in recent decades has not been confined to developing countries or to federations: there have been separatist movements in such countries as Spain and France, and pressures for devolution of functions to regional units in such countries as Italy and Britain.

Given these dual pressures throughout the world, for larger political units capable of fostering economic development and improved security on the one hand, and for smaller political units more sensitive to their electorates and capable of expressing local distinctiveness on the other hand, it is not surprising that the federal solution should have considerable appeal. Federalism provides a technique of political organization that permits action by a common government for certain common purposes, together with autonomous action by regional units of government for purposes that relate to maintaining regional distinctiveness. Indeed, taking account of such federal and quasi-federal examples as Canada, the United States, Mexico, Brazil, Venezuela, Argentina, Austria, the Federal Republic of Germany, Switzerland, Yugoslavia, Czechoslovakia, the U.S.S.R., Australia, India, Malaysia, and Nigeria, one writer has calculated that more than a billion people in the world today live in countries that can be considered or claim to be federal.[5] Furthermore, many of these federations are clearly multinational in their composition. This suggests that perhaps the federal system of government has the advantage of allowing a close approximation to the multinational reality of the contemporary world, by reconciling the need for large-scale, political organization with the recognition and protection of ethnic, linguistic, or historically derived diversity.

Yet, experience since 1945 also makes it clear that federalism is not the panacea that many have imagined it to be. A number of post-war federal experiments have been abandoned or temporarily suspended.[6] The secession of Bangladesh from Pakistan, the separation of Singapore from Malaysia, the

Nigerian civil war, the dissolution of the Federation of the West Indies and of the Federation of Rhodesia and Nyasaland are examples. Even in such classical federations as the United States (1789), Switzerland (1848 and 1874), Canada (1867), and Australia (1901), which stand out among the more than one hundred independent countries of this world for the longevity of their constitutions, tension continues between the responsibilities appropriately concentrated at the central level of government and the degree of responsibility and autonomy left with the component regional governments. The pressures for interregional integration and regional self-expression have both been intensified by conditions in the contemporary world. The degree to which federal systems may be expected to accommodate or resolve these pressures, therefore, warrants examination.

CATALYSTS OF POLITICAL INTEGRATION

"Integration" refers to the condition of making whole or complete and to the process of bringing together parts. Political integration is the uniting of distinct groups, communities, or regions into a workable and viable political organization. As R.J. Jackson and M.B. Stein point out, if confusion is to be avoided, political integration must be distinguished from the concepts of national integration, economic integration, and social integration, each of which may contribute to political integration but is itself distinct.[7] The concept of national integration refers to the process or condition of uniting the parts of a nation, that community living within a territory that shares a common history, set of symbols, and subjective feelings that bind its members to one another. Political integration may be coterminous with national integration in the case of the nation-state, but it may be limited to a smaller sub-national unit or take the form of a wider, multinational political organization. Economic integration refers to the closer linking together of economies in a free trade area, a common market, or an economic union, but the degree to which economic integration involves the creation of integrative political organs may vary. Social integration must also be distinguished from political integration. Social integration refers to the process or condition of interrelating social institutions, such as family and kinship systems, the systems of voluntary associations, and all the other aspects of a society including its economic and political institutions so that they operate in a cohesive and interdependent fashion. Political integration refers to the process of unifying political institutions into a cohesive whole over time or a condition of political cohesion.

It should be noted that, defined in this way, political integration must also be differentiated from federation. Federation represents a particular form of political integration, one in which the components are brought together in a particular kind of political union, namely, one in which there are at least two autonomous but interdependent orders of government, central and regional, neither subordinate to the other. The relationship of federalism to political integration is a two-way one, requiring an analysis of the degree of prior political integration necessary before an effective federal system can be established, and the extent to which a federal system in turn can foster and facilitate continued or more effective political integration.

The analysis of the factors contributing to political integration in a given case would require an examination of (1) the background conditions, including (*a*) the degree of spill-over from pre-existing national, economic, and social links or integration among the components, (*b*) the proximity of the components, (*c*) the relative size and bargaining power of the component units, and (*d*) the complementarity of their élites; (2) the strength of the integrative motives present, including (*a*) the desires for security from external or internal threats, (*b*) the desires for utilitarian or economic benefits, and (*c*) the desires for a common identity; (3) the character of the integrative process itself in terms of (*a*) the character of the bargaining process, (*b*) the role of the leading élites, and (*c*) the timing and sequence of steps in the process of negotiation and unification.[8]

CATALYSTS OF REGIONALISM

The strongest catalyst for political integration into supranational political units during the latter half of the twentieth century has been increasing world-wide interdependence in an era when advances in technology and communications have made it difficult for even nation-states to be self-sufficient economically or to defend their own security. Paradoxically, it is the awareness of this tendency that has also encouraged a stronger regional consciousness within political systems. The growth of larger and more remote political structures, coupled with the increasing pervasiveness of large governmental structures and bureaucracies upon the life of citizens, has provoked a counter-reaction. In the name of the group as well as individual autonomy, people increasingly protest against big government, vast bureaucracy, over-taxation and over-regulation, mammoth unions, excessively large multi-versities, vast impersonal cities, and giant places of work. This seems to express a broadly felt need for deconcentration of institutional and impersonal power and more effective individual and group participation in the exercise of political power. In the words of Arthur Macmahon: "Modern man is oppressed by the sense of heavy organization and distant controls; he longs to resolve things into comprehensible and manageable portions."[9]

The heightened resistance to political integration and the demand for self-expression, dignity, and self-rule have been particularly virile where regional groups have been marked by differences of language, race, religion, social structure, and cultural tradition. As in Canada so in Switzerland, India, Pakistan, Malaysia, Nigeria, and Rhodesia and Nyasaland, linguistic, religious, and racial minorities, fearing discrimination at the hands of numerical majorities, have insisted upon regional autonomy as a way to preserve their distinct identities. Where that distinctiveness has appeared to be threatened, such regional groups often have turned to outright secession as the only sure defence against assimilation. Examples may be found in the insistence of the Muslems on the Indian sub-continent upon partition and the creation of Pakistan in 1947, the pressure by Bengali-speaking East Pakistanis for greater autonomy and eventually for an independent Bangladesh, the resentment of the Singapore Chinese at their second-class status in a Malaysia ruled by Malays resulting in the separation of Singapore in 1965, and the attempted secession of Eastern Nigeria to become Biafra.

Linguistic identity has been a particularly potent force for regionalism. This is not surprising since language differences often serve as barriers to communication. Moreover, a shared language provides a means of expression and communion, which is a most important ingredient in one's awareness of a social identity and a treasured heritage of a common past. Not surprisingly, any community governed through a language other than its own has usually felt disenfranchised. Significantly, linguistic regionalism has been a greater problem in societies that are industrial or are in the process of modernization as compared with primitive agrarian societies, because, in the former, official recognition of a language substantially affects careers and employment opportunities. Where different linguistic groups exist within a state, it would appear that conflict is particularly severe when members of different language groups are under unequal pressures to learn the languages of the others and when the direction or intensity of pressures to learn the other languages is changing.[10]

Other cultural factors can also be divisive. In Switzerland, for example, political divisions have as often followed confessional as linguistic lines and, in Ireland, ostensibly religious divisions have been explosive. Generally, pressures for regionalism have been strongest where differences of language, race, religion, and social institutions have reinforced rather than cut across each other, or where they have been associated with economic subordination. In Switzerland, where the division between Protestants and Catholics has cut across linguistic lines, cantonal alignments on political questions have tended to vary according to whether linguistic or religious considerations were at issue and, consequently, cantonal alignments have been less polarized than that between French and English-speaking Canadians.

Among other factors contributing to the intensity of regional consciousness within the contemporary world have been regional differences in degree of modernization. Within those regions that have lagged behind, these differences create resentment and fears of exploitation or domination by the more advanced regions.[11] Differences in degrees of modernization are also associated with regional differences in political ideology, outlook, or style,[12] and with regional differences in economic interests. And while regional economic differences may contribute to integration through the exchange of products across regional boundaries, they may also foster regional consciousness because of related differences in problems of production, types of exports, sources of foreign capital, and appropriate policies for the promotion of economic development. This tendency can be observed in the recent history of Pakistan and Malaysia as well as Canada. Furthermore, although a political union may bring economic gains to the union as a whole, economic integration may have not only "trade-creation" but also "trade-diversion" effects, which impose hardships and inequalities on some regions. As experience in both older federations like Canada and Australia and in newer ones like Nigeria and Pakistan has shown, regional disparities in wealth can be one of the most explosive forces politically, particularly when these disparities coincide with linguistic and cultural cleavages. Indeed, many ostensibly linguistic, racial, or cultural movements for greater regional autonomy or even political separation in countries such as Canada, India, Malaysia, and Nigeria have had strong economic undercurrents related to the struggle for jobs and economic opportunities.

Another form of disparity, unequal ability to influence central politics, has also often been an important factor contributing to resentment and heightened regional consciousness. In Canada, the distrust of central Canada in the western and Atlantic provinces and of Ontario by Quebec has been a fact of Canadian history and is a major current source of political friction. Such forces contributed to the disintegration of the West Indies Federation and to the splitting up or amalgamation of regional units in order to provide a better political balance in both Nigeria and Pakistan.

One should not neglect the impact upon regional consciousness of direct or indirect external influences. Quebec, Biafra, and the Jura in Switzerland provide powerful examples of the possible impact of direct encouragement of a regional separatist movement by a foreign government. External examples and precedents, particularly those offered by the recent march to political independence and full membership in the United Nations on the part of a large number of relatively small former colonial territories, have also provided encouragement to regional groups by indicating that ministates can survive on the world scene. While there may be some question about the real meaning of political or economic independence in many of these countries, the fact that in Africa alone there are some twenty-five independent states with populations less than that of Quebec has not been lost on that province.

This discussion suggests that if regionalism is to be understood, it must be examined not only in terms of the absence of factors encouraging political integration, but also in terms of those factors that encourage a regional consciousness. The analysis of the factors contributing to regional consciousness in a given case would appear to require an examination of (1) the background conditions, including (*a*) the relative weakness of conditions encouraging political integration, (*b*) the degree to which the particular region itself is internally homogeneous in language, religion, race, and culture, (*c*) the degree to which the particular region differs from neighbouring regions in language, religion, race, and culture, level of modernization, and economic development and political ideology or outlook, (*d*) the degree of disparity in relative wealth and influence within existing political institutions, and (*e*) the competitiveness of élites; (2) the strength of the immediate motives for regionalism, including (*a*) the desire to secure the distinctive features of the regional society against threats of assimilation, (*b*) the desire to preserve or enhance utilitarian or economic benefits for the regional group, and (*c*) the desire for a sense of regional identity or even nationhood; (3) the character of the process of devolution or separation in terms of (*a*) the character of the negotiating process (e.g., use of referenda, elections, guerilla campaigns, etc.), (*b*) the role of the leading regional élites, (*c*) the responses of associated regions, (*d*) the impact of direct and indirect external influences, and (*e*) the timing and sequence of steps in the process of devolution or separation.

THE BALANCE OF PRESSURES

Because people are simultaneously members of and feel loyalty to several groups and communities such as family, work group, professional association, church, ethnic or linguistic community, political movement, village or city, regional community, nation, supranational association, or global community, allegiance is usually dispersed among these groups rather than focused on only one of them to the exclusion of the others. Because people's attachments to these different groups or communities vary in intensity and over time, these loyalties are not mutually exclusive. It is possible for a strong integrative consciousness in a wider community to co-exist with an equally strong regional consciousness[13] or for both forces to be relatively weak.

Where one of these pressures is strong and the other weak, the result is likely to be relatively peaceful integration or disintegration. But where both forces exist in something approaching an equal balance, there is likely to be both competition for people's loyalties and conflict. Thus, supranational movements and institutions seek to gain support by their opposition to existing national divisions, and national states often seek to submerge regional interests in the wider national interest. Similarly, regional movements usually seek to gain support through opposition to existing or proposed political unions or associations. The establishment of large centralized empires or unitary states on the one hand, or of completely sovereign ministates on the other, assumes that wider political integration and regional self-expression are inevitably incompatible and in conflict. Movements to establish or experiment with federal or confederal unions, on the other hand, represent efforts to achieve a closer political approximation to the reality of the contemporary world in which increasing pressures for wider political integration and for regional diversity co-exist.

THE FEDERAL AND CONFEDERAL ALTERNATIVES

A desire to create political institutions capable of both expressing and facilitating the reconciliation of the demands for wider political integration and regional diversity, for unity without uniformity and diversity without anarchy, has led to a variety of federal and confederal proposals and experiments. In the spectrum of forms of political integration, they fall midway between the extremes of sovereign, independent, political units co-operating with each other and of unitary unions with all legal and political sovereignty confided exclusively in a central government.

The federal and confederal forms of political integration both represent compromises that attempt to link political units together in such a way that some governmental powers and functions are assigned to a large unit and others are retained by smaller constituent units. In common language, the terms ''federation'' and ''confederation'' are often used interchangeably. Indeed, the establishment of a federal system by the *British North America Act, 1867*, is regularly referred to by Canadians as ''Confederation,'' and the Swiss Constitution of 1874 is specifically entitled ''The federal constitution of the Swiss Confederation.'' Nevertheless, scholars have usually distinguished these as two significantly different forms. In the federal form as usually defined, the central and regional governments each possess autonomous authority assigned by a formal constitution, so that neither order of government is legally or politically subordinate to the other and each order of government is elected by and directly acts upon the electorate. A confederal political system is usually defined as one in which the central government derives its original authority from the constituent regional governments and is, therefore, legally and politically subordinate to them, and in which the institutions are composed predominantly of delegates appointed by the constituent regional governments. An economic association, when it has common organizing institutions, as in the case of the European Community,

---

SPECTRUM OF FORMS OF POLITICAL INTEGRATION

weak			decentralized	
central	co-operation	confederation	unitary	strong
institutions				central
	formal	federation	centralized	institutions
	association		unitary	

is in political terms a form of confederal organization in which the functions assigned by the participating states to the common institutions are limited mainly to economic co-operation and co-ordination. The Parti-Québécois proposal for sovereignty-association also clearly belongs in this category.

In distinguishing the alternative forms in the spectrum of political integration, three further points should be noted. First, within each of the categories, a wide range of variations is possible. Unitary systems may be administratively and politically centralized or decentralized. Among federal systems, the allocation of responsibilities to each order of government and the structure of central institutions may vary. Confederations too may differ in the powers assigned to the central agencies and the degree of control exercised over these central agencies by the member states. Economic associations may take the form of free trade areas, customs unions, common markets, monetary unions, or economic unions. Co-operation among independent states may be informal or involve treaties and may be limited or extensive.

Second, although the categories are distinct, they tend like colours in the spectrum to shade into each other, decentralized unitary systems bearing some similarities to centralized federal systems, decentralized federations to centralized confederations, and decentralized confederations to treaty alliances or associations.

Third, pragmatic statesmen and nation builders, unconcerned with the niceties of theories and more interested in the pragmatic value of institutions, have sometimes attempted ''mixed solutions'' or hybrids combining elements from different forms within a single political system. Indeed, a case in point is the *British North America Act*, which has been described by K.C. Wheare as ''quasi-federal'' because the central powers of reservation and disallowance of provincial legislation (for some time now unused) represent features characteristic of unitary systems.[14] Since dividing lines between these forms of political integration cannot always be drawn precisely, it may sometimes be necessary to describe an individual political system as ''predominently federal,'' ''predominently confederal,'' or ''predominently unitary,'' as the case may be.

Both the confederal and federal forms of political organization attempt to express and facilitate the concurrent demands for wider political integration and for autonomous regional diversity by establishing two orders of government. They attempt to do this in such a way that those functions on which there is general common agreement are performed by the common central agencies, and other functions on which there is no such interregional agreement are performed by the smaller autonomous regional units. It has been argued that this maximizes citizen satisfaction (or in its negative formulation, minimizes citizen frustration) by making possible the satisfaction of specific individual preferences by the particular level of government with the scale appropriate for satisfying that preference.[15] It has also been argued that by making possible autonomous diversity at the regional level, these forms of political integration reduce the extent of conflict and contention likely to occur at the centre.

The difference between the federal and confederal forms lies in the fact that in federal systems, the central institutions are free to exercise responsibilities assigned to them under the constitution in a direct relationship with the electorate, while in confederal systems the central agencies, operating as delegates of the regional governments, are dependent upon them for agreement to common policies. Attempts to judge the relative effectiveness of the two approaches suffer from the limitation that examples of political confederations are relatively rare today, although the confederal principle is alive in such interstate economic associations as the European Community and, in a more general sense, in the United Nations itself.

It has generally been argued that the advantage of a confederal form of political integration is that it enables regional units to retain ultimate control of their own destiny. Because central agencies are composed of regional delegates and because on major issues central decisions are subject to an ultimate veto by regional governments, the chance of particular regional interests being overriden is limited, thus reducing a region's sense of insecurity for its autonomy and diversity. The disadvantages of the confederal form relate largely to the difficulty of obtaining agreement upon policies among all the component regional governments. Common action by central agencies is likely to be limited to areas where all or an overwhelming number of regional governments are agreed, thus limiting central effectiveness. For instance, agreement upon any extensive redistribution or equalization of resources among component regions in order to counterbalance the trade diversion effects of a common market or to reduce disparities in regional wealth is usually difficult to obtain under such conditions. Furthermore, political confederations have historically been marked by instability. It should not be forgotten that both the United States and Switzerland abandoned confederal forms of political organization because of their inability to deal adequately with common problems, and that each now looks back on the adoption of a federal system as a turning point in its effective development. Furthermore, the slowness of the movement of the European Community toward its original objectives and the limited impetus for European political integration, which could develop from functional co-ordination, offer indications of the difficulties faced by confederations.

But while confederal approaches have their limitations, federal solutions do not provide panaceas. They have the advantage that their central institutions, in the areas assigned to them by the constitution, are likely to be able to operate more decisively. Consequently, they are also in a stronger position to redistribute resources and reduce regional disparities. There is historical evidence that federations can be stable forms of political integration. While it is true that a significant number of the newer federations established since 1945 have disintegrated, it is also true that the United States (1789), Switzerland (1848), Canada (1867), Australia (1901), and the Federal Republic of Germany (1950) provide significant examples of the potential stability of federal systems.[16] Moreover, in the last of these cases, the relative effectiveness of the Bonn Constitution, by contrast with the Weimar Republic, suggests that constitutional engineering can have a significant impact on political behaviour. The institutional framework shapes and channels the activities of the electorate, political parties, organized interest groups, bureaucracies, and informal élites, and therefore can contribute to the moderation or accentuation of political conflict. While these federations have each undergone periods of stress, it would appear that they have generally succeeded over time in reconciling internal demands for both unity and diversity. Indeed, it is characteristic of them that, in practice, their impact has been to encourage not only "nation building" but also "province building."[17]

Such achievements have not been without a price, however. As critics have pointed out, the constitutional distribution of powers between two orders of government has meant that federal systems have been marked by complexity, legalism, rigidity, conservatism, and expense in their operation. It has even been argued that because federations are conservative political systems representing delicate balances of internal power, they tend to be "closed" toward the outside world and less open to even wider supranational associations.[18] These liabilities have usually been accepted, however, as the necessary price for achieving a wider political integration that is more effective than a confederal organization and provides greater protection for regional interests than a unitary system.

There is, of course, no ultimate or ideal form of political integration appropriate to all political circumstances. As the earlier analysis of factors contributing to demands for political integration and for regional autonomy inferred, the particular balance between these demands will vary in different countries and over time. A federal organization, therefore, will not by any means always be an appropriate solution. Its appropriateness would appear to lie in those instances where the existence and vigour of forces that press for both wider unity and for autonomous regional diversity are relatively balanced. But even in such cases, the effectiveness of a federal system may depend upon the particular form that it takes.

THE VARIETY OF FEDERAL SYSTEMS

Whether a federal system can, in a particular instance, accommodate and reconcile the demands for interregional or supranational political integration and for autonomous regional diversity will also depend upon the particular institutional structure of that federal system. While certain essential features are common to all federal systems, in fact no two federations have been absolutely identical. Each federation has been in a sense a unique experiment, combining in its own distinctive way a particular regional structure, distribution of powers, arrangement for intergovernmental co-operation, organization of central government, and protection for the supremacy of the constitution. Thus, in assessing the effectiveness of a federal political system, it is necessary to consider the particular form of its institutions and the degree to which they appropriately express and reconcile the demands of the multiregional society on which it is based.

The essential features common to federal systems, to systems within which authority is distributed between two co-ordinate orders of government, are the following:

1. Two orders of government (central and regional) existing in their own right under the constitution

2. The co-ordinacy in legal and political status of the two orders of government in the sense that neither order is subordinate to the other

3. Direct election to each order of government (rather than indirectly through the other order of government) and direct action (through legislation and taxation) by each government upon its own electorate

4. A formal distribution of autonomous legislative and executive authority and of sources of revenue between the two orders of government

5. A written constitution that defines the jurisdiction and resources of the two orders of government and that is not unilaterally amendable in its fundamental provisions by only one order of government

6. A process for adjudicating disputes relating to respective governmental powers and for interpreting the constitution, a process that usually involves a supreme court or a specialized constitutional court but that may take the form of the electorate acting through a referendum

7. Processes and institutions to facilitate intergovernmental consultation and accommodation

8. Central institutions structured to ensure sensitivity to regional and minority interests (usually involving a bicameral central legislature and regional representativeness in the central executive and bureaucracy, although the latter may depend upon convention).

Within such a basic federal framework, there is considerable scope for variation in each of the elements that go to make up a federal system, and these variations will have a critical impact upon the effectiveness of the federal system. In considering these various elements separately, we should remember, however, that within a given system they must be interrelated: for example, the form of central institutions that is appropriate or the form of intergovernmental consultative procedures that is suitable may be related to the scope and nature of functions assigned to each order of government.

The number, absolute size, and relative size of the regional units of government are important variables, which affect the relative capacity of the units to perform functions and which determine their relative influence in relation to each other and to the central government. For instance, the tiny cantons of Switzerland (twenty-three of them in a total federal population no more than Ontario's), the relative bargaining power in relation to the central government of Australia's six states by comparison with the United States' fifty, and the extreme asymmetry in size and wealth and hence governmental capacity of Ontario in relation to Prince Edward Island illustrate the way in which the political balance within a federation may be affected by the number and size of its regional governmental units.

The distribution of functions and resources has varied considerably from federation to federation. In some, the legislative and executive responsibilities coincide within each level of government, but in Switzerland and the Federal Republic of Germany, the pattern is one of relatively centralized legislative authority and constitutionally decentralized administrative authority. There is considerable variation in the extent to which most powers have been assigned exclusively to one level of government or the other as in Canada and Switzerland, or the extent to which numerous areas have been placed under concurrent jurisdiction as in Australia and West Germany. Federations vary as well in the allocation of the residual authority, which in Canada and India, unlike most other federations, is assigned to the central government. The extent to which quasi-unitary unilateral powers are assigned to the central government to override provincial autonomy in emergencies or under certain specified conditions varies also, such powers being particularly extensive in the Indian and Canadian federations. Federations have varied considerably too in the specific legislative fields and financial resources assigned to each order of government, with the result that there is a considerable range in degrees of centralization or decentralization. On one simple measure alone a comparative study of state public expenditure as a percentage of total public expenditure (after revenue transfers) showed a range from 17 per cent in Malaya and 26 per cent in the United States to 58 per cent in India, 62 per cent in Switzerland, and 97 per cent in the short-lived West Indies Federation. Between these two groups were to be found Australia, West Germany, Canada, Pakistan, and Nigeria.[19]

It would appear that where the distribution of authority and resources has failed to reflect accurately the aspirations for political integration and for regional autonomy, there have been pressures for a shift in the balance of powers or in extreme cases even for abandoning the federal experiment, as happened in overcentralized Pakistan or the ineffectual West Indies. A factor that has made the finding of the appropriate balance more difficult in the contemporary world is that a simple compromise between economic centralization and cultural regionalization is no longer a realistic policy in the way that it may have been a century or two ago. In most multicultural federations, as in Canada, regional, linguistic, or cultural groups have developed a deep-rooted anxiety that, because of the pervasive impact of public economic policy upon all aspects of society, centralized fiscal and economic policies aiming at the rapid development of an integrated economy will undermine their cultural distinctiveness and opportunities for employment in culturally congenial conditions. In the face of such concerns, most contemporary federations have found it necessary to develop interlocking central-regional responsibility over a wide range of functions, particularly in economic matters. This has been especially so in the sharing of financial resources because of the need to match the financial resources of regional governments to their constitutional responsibilities, and because of the importance of redistributing resources through equalization schemes in order to reduce disparities in wealth, which would otherwise become a source of resentment and severe internal tension.

Asymmetry in the size and wealth of their regional units has led some federations such as Malaysia, India, Pakistan, and Rhodesia and Nyasaland to experiment with giving some regional governments more autonomy than others. A similar solution has been proposed from time to time in the form of a ''special status'' for Quebec within Canada. Experience elsewhere suggests, however, that while a moderate asymmetry in the formal constitutional authority of regional governments can be tolerated and may indeed better reflect political reality, major differences in degrees of regional autonomy have generally fostered, rather than reduced, tension. The most notable example is that of the brief membership of Singapore within the Malaysian Federation.

Because it is within the central institutions that accommodation among the different regional viewpoints must be arrived at for policies relating to the exercise of those responsibilities assigned to the central government, the character of the central institutions and their ability to generate a sense of community for the federation as a whole are particularly important. Critical here is how regional groups and communities are represented in the central legislature, executive, civil service, political parties, and life of the capital city. Where such groups are inadequately represented, as in the case of the East Pakistanis, the Singapore Chinese, the Jamaicans, or the black Africans of Rhodesia and Nyasaland, the resulting alienation has culminated eventually in separation.

A particularly significant variation among federations, affecting both the manner in which regional interests are accommodated and reconciled in the formulation of central policies and the character of intergovernmental relations, is the extent to which the principle of the ''separation of powers'' between the executive and legislature is incorporated. In federations such as the United States with its presidential system and Switzerland with its collegial system, it has been possible to establish second chambers in which the states are equally represented and which are equal in constitutional power to the chamber in which representation is by population. Furthermore, the framework of checks and balances within their central institutions has in most periods encouraged the search by politicians and political parties for compromises because of the variety of points at which minority groups could otherwise block action. Furthermore, the diffusion of authority within each order of government has enabled the development of many points of contact and interpenetration between the two orders of government resulting in what Morton Grodzins has labelled ''marble cake'' federalism.[20]

In those federations where the central governments are organized along parliamentary lines, such as Canada, Australia, and most of the newer Commonwealth federations, central cabinets with majority legislative support have been able more easily to undertake rapid and effective action, but at the price of placing complete sovereignty in the hands of a parliamentary majority with few institutional checks upon it. Invariably in such systems, the second chambers, intended to be particularly representative of regional communities, are weaker than the first chambers. Parliamentary systems with their strict party discipline thus put the responsibility for reconciling political conflicts and for aggregating support from diverse regional and cultural groups more directly upon the internal organization and processes of the political parties themselves. Consequently, when in such systems parties have become primarily regional in their bases, the parliamentary federations have been prone to instability, as in Pakistan before 1958 and Nigeria before 1966. It is not surprising, therefore, that the pattern of the results of the Canadian federal election of February 1980 and the resulting underrepresentation of the western provinces in a majority government should have quickly become a matter of concern. The parliamentary form of government has also affected the character of intergovernmental relations. For example, in Canada and Australia, the dominance of the parliamentary cabinets at both levels has made these executive bodies the focus of relations between the two orders of government. This ''executive federalism,'' as Donald Smiley has described it, seems often to produce intergovernmental relations that operate in a manner not unlike international diplomacy. The result in these instances is a ''layer cake'' federalism that contrasts with the ''marble cake'' character of non-parliamentary federations.[21]

Other variables in the federal structure also affect the character of its operation and its effectiveness. These include the particular form of the processes and institutions through which intergovernmental consultation and co-operation are facilitated—a field in which the Australian Loans Council, Commonwealth Grants Commission, and the West German Bundesrat have been interesting innovations. Also significant is the structure of the judicial system, the supreme court or constitutional court, and the use of other devices, such as the Swiss use of the legislative referendum, for adjudicating disputes related to respective governmental powers. The impact of judicial review upon the way in which a federal system protects the interests of minorities is itself affected by whether the constitution includes a specification of entrenched fundamental rights limiting the scope of both central and state action. The procedures for constitutional amendment and the inclusion of provisions for the delegation of responsibilities from one level of government to the other affect the extent to which the federation is sufficiently flexible and adaptable to respond to changing conditions over time. Here federations have to find a balance between providing sufficient constitutional rigidity to ensure the confidence of regional communities in the ability of the federal structure to safeguard their interests, and providing sufficient flexibility to be able to respond to changes in social and economic conditions.

CONCLUSIONS

This paper has attempted to point to the great driving forces that, for a variety of reasons, have produced powerful pressures both for the interregional or supranational political integration and for more autonomous regional entities. In the search for the middle ground that would permit the mutual accommodation of these pressures for unity and diversity, the federal form of organization, in spite of its complexities and rigidities, appears to provide a dynamic political technique that permits perhaps the closest political approximation to contemporary reality. The degree to which a federal system can accommodate this reality will depend, however, upon the extent to which the particular form of federal institutions adopted or evolved gives full expression to the demands of the particular society in question. Ultimately federalism is a pragmatic, prudential technique whose continued applicability may depend upon further innovations in its institutional variables.

Federal systems are no panacea but they may be necessary as the only way of combining, through representative institutions, the benefits of both unity and diversity. Experience indicates that federations, both old and new, have been difficult countries to govern. But then, that is usually why they have federal political institutions.

NOTES

[1] H.J. Laski, "The Obsolescence of Federalism," *The New Republic* 98 (3 May 1939), p. 367.

[2] Clifford Geertz, ed., *Old Societies and New States: The Quest for Modernity in Asia and Africa* (London: Collier-Macmillan, 1963), p. 108, quoted by R.J. Jackson and M.B. Stein, *Issues in Comparative Politics* (New York: St. Martin's, 1971), p. 119.

[3] Ivo Duchachek, *Comparative Federalism: The Territorial Dimension of Politics* (New York: Holt, Rinehart and Winston, 1970), p. 2.

[4] *Ibid.*, p. 69.

[5] Gilles Lalande (transl. by J. LaPierre), *In Defence of Federalism: A View from Quebec* (Toronto: McClelland and Stewart, 1978), pp. 11-12. See also Duchachek, *op. cit.*, pp. 195-98.

[6] See R.L. Watts, "Survival or Disintegration," in *Must Canada Fail?* edited by Richard Simeon (Montreal: McGill-Queen's University Press, 1977), pp. 42-60; and T.M. Franck *et al.*, eds., *Why Federations Fail: An Inquiry into the Requisites for Successful Federalism* (New York: New York University Press, 1968).

[7] Jackson and Stein, *op. cit.*, pp. 114-15.

[8] For interesting analytical frameworks for the study of unification, see A. Etzioni, *Political Unification* (Huntingdon, N.Y.: Krieger, 1965); J.S. Nye, Jr., *International Regionalism* (Boston: Little, Brown, 1968), pp. 333-49; and P.E. Jacob and J.V. Toscano, eds., *The Integration of Political Communities* (Philadelphia: Lippencott, 1964), pp. 1-45.

[9] Arthur W. Macmahon, *Federalism: Mature and Emergent* (New York: Doubleday, 1955), p. 32.

[10] Based on a study of linguistic problems in Switzerland, Czechoslovakia, Alsace-Lorraine, and North Schleswig by Walter B. Simon, quoted in Duchachek, *op. cit.*, p. 308.

[11] This was a factor in prepartition India and in Northern Nigeria and contributed to the "Quiet Revolution" in Quebec.

[12] Malaysia, Nigeria, and Pakistan have presented obvious examples among the newer federations, and to some extent this has been a factor too in Canada.

[13] Note the counter-separatist slogan of the Quebec Liberal Party: "We choose Quebec AND Canada."

[14] K.C. Wheare, *Federal Government* (London: Oxford University Press, 1963), pp. 18-19.

[15] J.R. Pennock, "Federal and Unitary Government—Disharmony and Frustration," *Behavioural Science* 4 (April 1959): 147-57.

[16] Geoffrey Sawer, *Modern Federalism* (London: Watts, 1969), pp. 179-80.

[17] See, for instance, E.R. Black and A.C. Cairns, "A Different Perspective on Canadian Federalism," *Canadian Public Administration* 9 (March 1966): 27-44.

[18] David Mittrany, "The Prospect of Integration: Federal or Functional?" in *International Regionalism*, edited by J.S. Nye, Jr. (Boston: Little, Brown, 1968), pp. 43-73.

[19] R.L. Watts, *Administration in Federal Systems* (London: Hutchinson, 1970), p. 143, Table 2.

[20] Morton Grodzins, *The American System: A New View of Government in the United States* (Chicago: Rand McNally, 1966).

[21] D.V. Smiley, *Canada in Question: Federalism in the Seventies* (Toronto: McGraw-Hill Ryerson, 1976), Chapter 3. See also Richard Simeon, *Federal-Provincial Diplomacy: The Making of Recent Policy in Canada* (Toronto: University of Toronto Press, 1972).

Chapter Two

The Crisis of the West European State

by
Gordon Smith

Is Western Europe afflicted by a "crisis of the state"? There are many who would say that it is not, and they might add that we should concentrate on particular problems rather than raise issues dealing with such an imponderable as the future of "the state." This view has merit; it is temptingly easy to assume that a general crisis exists merely because descriptions of "ungovernability" have become commonplace. Specific cases—the permanent crisis of government in Italy, the violence of Basque separatism, the malaise of industrial relations in Britain, linguistic fragmentation in Belgium, the "colonial war" in Northern Ireland—are all brought together to produce the fallacy of aggregation.

Nonetheless, the evidence of diverse pressures upon the state is not easily to be dismissed. These pressures all have implications for the authority of the state, whether they take a dramatic form as with terrorism, or are almost imperceptible as in the impact of supranational forces. Yet we face a difficulty in comprehending the nature of these pressures. Is it feasible to try to relate the various types and levels of problem in a coherent way? They all find a focus in the state, but can we also disentangle their separate effects?

This chapter is an attempt to answer these questions.[1] It does so by examining some of the leading features of the modern state and by showing how the cumulative effect of changing conditions may be altering the West European state in significant ways. To advance the argument, it will be necessary to isolate from a larger body of theory those features of the state which appear currently relevant and to apply them separately to developments in Western Europe. We can represent the leading attributes in summary form as follows:

1. The conception of the state as a legal and physical entity
2. The relationship of the state to society
3. The sources of legitimacy supporting the state.

Once the three perspectives have been outlined and examined in their West European context, it will be easier to trace possible "lines of adjustment." The advantage of this approach is that whether we are sifting

21

evidence of "crisis" or looking at forms of accommodation, a theoretical coherence can be maintained. The contemporary state does not face a single, overwhelming crisis, but the pressures may lead to a substantial redefinition of its characteristic features.

THE DECLINE OF THE "HARD SHELL" STATE

The view of the state as "a legal and physical entity" is another way of expressing the theory of sovereignty and the recognition by others of a state's existence in the international community. Essentially, it is a rendering of the state in terms of law, but the concept can be understood in non-legal terms as well. The description used by John Herz is particularly apt: the state is seen as providing a "hard shell" towards its external environment.[2] We can appreciate that any state must seek to present a cohesive front to the outside world.

In a formal sense, the claim to sovereignty is the most important factor in maintaining cohesion, but there are other ingredients in the hard shell. The principal idea is that of the state as representing the prime unit of physical security and the guardian of territorial integrity. The territorial aspect is, of course, vital, since without control over its own territory, a state's very existence is in jeopardy. A second ingredient is the state considered as the guarantor of economic autonomy. This economic function expresses the ability of the state to control its destiny in a world where the growth of trade, and the international economy generally, tends to undermine its competence and authority.

Although the role of "guardian and guarantor" is basic to a state's performance, in practice a wide range of variation is possible. Outright failure would probably mean the demise of the state, but there is a large intermediate band between success and failure. Those states that are able to preserve a hard shell prove to be "adequate," whilst others show varying degrees of inadequacy. The inadequate state may well survive and even prosper, but it is apparent that one of its central characteristics is made redundant.

It is possible to argue that the states of Western Europe have moved furthest away from the "physical" requirements of adequacy, at least in comparison with their historical position. This *relative* shift has been dramatic in the speed with which the major West European powers have had to forfeit their independent provision for physical security. Ultimately, they all rely on the protective shield of the United States, and that is so whether the individual states concede their position through membership in the North Atlantic Treaty Organisation or whether they formally remain outside multilateral defence agreements. It is true that they still have the ability to protect themselves from their immediate neighbours within Western Europe, but the likelihood of having to do so is remote. In effect, the states have lost a substantial part of their protective function, and this loss puts them in an entirely different category from other states—especially the super-powers and the host of new or emergent states that still have to maintain intact their *individual* capabilities.

A parallel decline is evident in the economic realm, although the reasons are different and the evidence, less conclusive. The states of Western Europe are particularly susceptible to the needs of advanced industrial society and developed capitalist systems. Western Europe has proved especially responsive to economic pressures, in part because the need for wider markets conflicts with the restrictive nature of the numerous state boundaries. The creation of the European Community can be seen as a response to the growing inadequacy of the West European state. However, too great an emphasis on the European Community should be avoided. Several states are quite able to maintain their position without becoming members, and the trends of economic transnationalism, although they have political implications, need not result in a formal, institutional expression as is the case with the European Community.[3] There is thus no imperative reason for supposing that economic inadequacy should result in the formation of a new political community.

MOVEMENTS IN THE STATE/SOCIETY LINE

The second attribute of the state concerns its internal functioning. Various means can be used to portray the relationship of state to society, and the idea of a "line" separating or distinguishing the two, which G. Poggi introduces in his formulation of a "state/society line," is only one possibility.[4] It may be misleading to imply that a single notional line could represent the complexities of involvement between state and society, even the interpenetration of the two. Any line would have to be drawn differently according to the nature of the relationship involved. In this discussion we shall be concerned only with the economic relationships and the associated provision of "social welfare."

Movements in this line have resulted partly from the requirements of the economy itself, which lead to several forms of increasing state regulation and intervention. One manifestation of this is summed up in the idea of "corporatism," which typically is seen as a partnership between the state and the private sector.[5] In one version of "state corporatism," the state assumes a leading role in the *economy*, moving from being the supporter of the private sector to a position of effective control over a range of decisions formerly taken by individual firms. Although the principle of private ownership is maintained, the private sector becomes increasingly dependent on the state for its continued survival. Whatever evaluation is made of the theory of corporatism, the increasing responsibilities of the state stand out as the cardinal feature. Even though the line is a blurred one, corporatism signifies the interpenetration of the state and sectors of society—to the detriment of pluralism and the representative institutions of liberal democracy.

To this pressure for state involvement has to be added the demands from society that lead directly to increasing state intervention. It is in the nature of liberal democracy that social and welfare claims are given maximum weight. Precisely because the liberal state is in no position to reject the claims made upon its resources, it sometimes appears in danger of being overwhelmed by them. Once shouldered, the commitments are not easily shed, and the external view of the inadequate state may have an internal equivalent in the form of an "over-extended" state.

Governments ignore social demands and expectations at their peril, for they must ultimately face the consequences of party competition. This is a general phenomenon of liberal democracies, especially where a centre or catch-all party is predominant. The need to appeal to the same sectors of the electorate and the absence of competing ideologies set a framework that restricts the realization if not the development of strong policy alternatives. The state is caught on a rail of expanding commitment.

Western Europe differs from the model of catch-all party competition in a significant way.[6] Older party traditions have proved remarkably durable, as have the parties with which they are associated. In this respect, the traditions of social democracy are of overriding importance.[7] Possibly they no longer represent the aspirations of an underprivileged working class or the dynamic appeal of a social movement, but they do correspond to the demands of the most important section of the electorate—the organized labour movement. The traditions continue to enshrine the values of collectivism which, for want of a practicable alternative, are indelibly marked with the imprint of state intervention and usually with state centralism as well: the purposive control of collective effort.

The social democratic component of West European party systems (to which, for this purpose, the Communist parties should be added) by no means controls even a majority of governments. Yet the collectivist spirit is pervasive, fostered by the terms of party competition on the one hand, and by the administrative traditions of European governments on the other,[8] although a belief in the virtues of state direction and centralization shares nothing with the ideals of collectivist equality. Some of the consequences of the West European version of "over-extension" will become apparent when one looks at the third ingredient of the state: the sources of its legitimacy.

POPULAR LEGITIMACY AND THE LIBERAL STATE

To say that there are several sources of legitimacy for the state implies that we can move from the legal connotations of "rightful authority" and sovereignty to the wider connections involved in ideas of "loyalty to the state" and "popular legitimacy." As a loose expression, one might refer to support for the political system as a whole, and it is apparent that reasons for giving support will be various and subject to change.[9] Whilst the basic quality of legality must be present, at least to the extent that a modern state is founded on a belief in ''rational-legal'' authority, by itself that characteristic may prove insufficient as a sanction or as the ground for strong attachment.

One basis for allegiance is located in the symbolic capacity of ''the nation'' and especially its conjunction with the state in the idea of the ''nation-state.'' The appeal to national feeling rests on the presence of real and common affinities—a shared history, language, and culture. But there are mythical, even arbitrary elements as well, which E. Kedourie succinctly expressed in his definition: ''Nationalism is a *doctrine* invented in Europe at the beginning of the nineteenth century.''[10] If nations can create states, states can also create nations.

The implications of this are important. Nationalism and national feeling do not have a completely independent existence, like a kind of Sleeping Beauty simply waiting to be aroused. The sentiments that underpin loyalty to the nation-state depend upon the performance and effectiveness of the state beyond the record of successive governments. It is here that the particular qualities of the contemporary state become relevant. If a description of their ''inadequacy'' and ''over-extension'' is to any extent true, then the bases of attachment may wear thin or, alternatively, substantially change. One possibility is that strong national feeling may be replaced by a cosmopolitan independence, a civilized *Weltbürgertum*. Another is that new loyalties will arise in direct conflict with the nation-state: instead of the state being the focus of uncritical commitment, more local affinities are discovered.

The relevance of these tendencies can be seen in the consequences of the decline of the hard-shell state in Western Europe. If loyalty to the nation-state weakens as its external functions become redundant, will there be a transfer of attachments to a supranational level? In this context, the potential of the European Community is of obvious importance, but its deficiencies are also considerable. First, the Community is not a supranational counterpart of the nation-state in that it has neither inherited nor assumed the task of providing physical security—that opportunity was relinquished in the failure to set up a European Defence Community in the 1950s. Second, the process of integration has had an ambiguous effect on the position of the member states. Whatever plans the ''European idealists'' may have had to relegate these states to a subordinate status, they remain the key intermediaries and retain a locus of authority in the Council of Ministers and the European Council, which none of the other Community institutions can match. Indeed, the framework of the Community encourages bilateral and multilateral links as much as supranational ones. Third, the emphasis on economic integration has heightened awareness of competing national interests. Those interests are not reconciled by evidence of an increasing imbalance of economic strength, a disparity that will become greater with the admission of Greece, Portugal, and Spain. Nor has the Community proved convincing in moving much beyond the primary, "negative" stage of integration—the removal of barriers—to a "positive" one that might promote a European identity of interest and modify the imbalances, or at least reduce their political significance.

For all these reasons, the prospects of the Community forming the basis of a supranational allegiance are dim, at least in the foreseeable future. It is no surprise at all that public awareness, and even knowledge, of the European Community should remain at a low level. Public indifference was confirmed by the first direct election to the European Assembly.[11] Whatever the tactical successes of that body—for instance, in initially rejecting the Community's 1980 budget—the activities of shadowy "transnational" parties are no substitute for the red meat of domestic politics.[12]

It is apparently more profitable to look within the states themselves for a resolution of the problems of legitimacy. It is also clear that there are special difficulties facing states in maintaining their internal level of support. The shift in the state/society line has had a paradoxical effect: in an era during which the state has become almost hypersensitive to the expressed needs of society, manifestations of thwarted expectation and disillusionment have become rife. This reaction, however, is explicable if account is taken of the built-in "escalating mechanism" of liberal democracy, and it becomes part of the syndrome of the over-extended state.

The paradox can be formulated in an alternative way: signs of a mounting problem of "governability" have become evident at a time when the basis of legitimate authority has been altering—away from traditional sources towards a "social-eudemonic" type, in which the state is legitimized through its economic and social welfare capabilities.[13] The description of "the distributive state" may be relevant, but it implies a kind of neutral arbitration when, in fact, the state becomes enmeshed in a web of competing and rising obligations.

The argument favoured here is that "ungovernability" and over-extension are closely related and that their combination represents a "delegitimizing" process for the state.[14] Yet it has to be admitted that the ungovernability thesis is extremely vague in its application; it is employed to explain everything from problems of "law and order," through the ruthless pressing of sectional economic interests, more general signs of discontent in society, to the turmoils associated with regional movements. Even though these phenomena may yield a common result in the apparent embarrassment, even the helplessness, of governments in facing one challenge to their authority after another, the profusion of claims by "minorities" is offset almost entirely by the continuing quiescence of "majorities." Upon reflection, it becomes evident that ungovernability in its literal sense has little relevance to the real situation in Western Europe.

Where the description does have force is in bringing attention to the problems of a state engaged in a range of complex activities, faced with difficulties of co-ordination, and increasingly dependent on the co-operation of a host of social groups over which it is unable to exercise effective control. These groups are able to push demands, to exercise a power of veto, or simply to act in defiance of governmental authority. Those concerned may not be intent on challenging the legitimacy of the state, but the erosive effect is nevertheless the same.[15] On occasion, there may be a danger of explosion, which threatens the stability of a whole society, but that outcome is unlikely. After all, we are considering a group of countries that have highly stable political systems. If anything, this stability has increased along with the wholesale decline of anti-system movements, whether on the Right or the Left; this decline and the advent of ''Eurocommunism'' at least indicate that there is little electoral appeal in following a revolutionary strategy.

Ungovernability, then, is better reserved for describing the vitiation of authority rather than its overthrow. It is also of use in depicting popular attitudes towards government. Richard Rose uses the term ''civic indifference'' to portray this possible trend:

> An indifferent citizen does not need to take up arms against a regime; he simply closes his eyes and ears to what it commands. The apathetic masses may sit out power struggles within government, and turn the victor's position into a hollow triumph by shutting out a new government behind a wall of indifference.[16]

As we have seen, the state has already experienced a weakening of one source of its appeal through its changing external status. If that loss is compounded by internal apathy, then the consequences for legitimacy are profound. The two developments may have occurred independently of one another, but they find a common expression in a renewed concern with the idea of ''territory'' as a focus of popular loyalty.

THE TERRITORIAL DIMENSION

One of the remarkable features of Western Europe in recent years has been the upsurge of claims at a regional level for varying degrees of autonomy or self-rule. In many cases, the demands have been modest and peacefully expressed, but in others they have amounted to separatist movements and verged on civil war. It is important to note that there has been no general challenge to the constitutional integrity of the European states: the total incidence of what we may conveniently call ''substate'' nationalism has been small, and many West European countries have been entirely unaffected by it. Furthermore, the attractions of such movements wane as well as wax. Only a few years ago, forecasts of the imminent break-up of the United Kingdom had to be taken seriously, but now—in the aftermath of the 1979 election—they are more likely to be derided.[17]

How should this uneven incidence and intensity be interpreted? One explanation is fairly obvious: claims for freedom from the policies of a central government will be made most effectively in areas where there are strong ethnic, cultural, or linguistic affinities. To some extent, these represent outcroppings of old identities that were submerged by the rise of the nation-state. But why should this ''renaissance'' of territorial minorities occur at the present time?[18] Frequently such movements are particularly active in regions that are remote from central government. Those regions are probably the first to appreciate the negative effects of a growing centralization and show the sharpest reaction.

In fact, the rise or regeneration of a local consciousness need not be linked specifically to pre-existing affinities. The pressure may come from real or perceived economic and related grievances, crystallizing around rediscovered identities. Once the latter have been revived, they can become a force in their own right, irrespective of changing economic fortunes. Equally, they may be deflected by other currents, typically being drawn back into the conventional party battle and the familiar Left/Right dichotomy.

This presentation helps to explain the uneven nature of regional movements, although the renewed significance of ''political territory'' within the state can be accounted for in another way as well. The earlier reference to the external inadequacy of the state becomes relevant here. The diminishing need to provide direct physical security against a potential aggressor has an immediate and potentially unsettling effect on the position of frontier regions. More generally, one can say that the declining territorial significance of the state allows other, and especially sub-national, forces to assert their own claims. Thus we can see that the territorial dimension is important for the question of legitimacy, not as a factor in its own right but as one which may be used by the state or which may be available to those who reject the authority of the existing state. In brief, if there is a crisis of the state, then no solution can ignore the territorial element.

Before turning to ways in which adjustments might be made, it may be useful to summarize the relationships involved in the pressures on the contemporary state in diagram form.

PRESSURES ON STATE LEGITIMACY

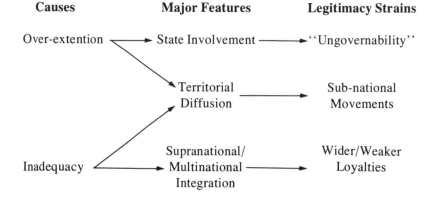

Causes	Major Features	Legitimacy Strains
Over-extention	State Involvement	''Ungovernability''
	Territorial Diffusion	Sub-national Movements
Inadequacy	Supranational/ Multinational Integration	Wider/Weaker Loyalties

MAJOR TYPES OF SOLUTION

Any solution to the state's loss of legitimacy must concentrate on remedying the deficit attributable to one or more of the factors examined. Thus one possibility, probably an unrealistic one, would be to seek to restore the adequacy of the state, to sever all multinational and supranational links, and to pursue a policy of isolation and autarky. Albania serves as a good example of this approach. If the people could be convinced that such a strategy was unavoidable or desirable, it is conceivable that they would rally to the cause of the beleaguered state.

A second approach focuses attention on the problem of over-extension. It involves an attempt to extricate the state by redrawing the state/society line. Beyond the belief that a withdrawal of the state in itself would result in general economic benefits for society, this solution contains an important assumption about legitimacy: less government means more respected government. This resurrected "anti-statist" philosophy has yet to be fully tested in Western Europe. However, by bringing a fresh injection of ideology into political debate and through head-on conflict with the doctrine of collectivism, this new-style conservatism faces the risk of exposing social cleavages that had healed over. The resulting polarization, far from enhancing the legitimacy of the state, could simply weaken it still further.

Other solutions leave the issue of the state/society line aside by aiming instead at some kind of "restructuring" of the state. A common objective is to secure an effective dispersion of the state's power on the grounds that it is the concentration of such power, rather than its extent, which leads to social discontent.

One possibility within this second approach has been summed up in the slogan of "democratization." It is a call for "more democracy" and is directed against the view that while the state and its apparatus may be politically responsible and thus democratically controlled, it should be protected from the immediate and direct influences of society. Since the enormous extension of state activity has not resulted in any fundamental reform of the traditional model of a unified and "self-sufficient" state machine, the remedy is not to "bolster up" the legitimacy of the state, but to supplant it. In principle, the argument for a democratization of the state avoids a simple political translation, but it is closely associated with familiar ideologies of the Left, just as anti-statism is linked with those of the Right. There are direct connections between the ideas of democratization and those of anarcho-syndicalism, as well as Marxist views of the repressive character of the state.[19] It is also a small step to take from democratizing the state to democratizing society, with the identical aim of dispersing power. It is evident that any attempt to restructure the state must have ideological implications and they will lead to a strong polarization in society. But does this objection apply with the same force to "territorial" solutions?

ANSWERS IN DECENTRALIZATION?

Admittedly, proposals for substantial decentralization of power can lead to just as much bitter debate as any other form of restructuring. If there are firm centralist traditions, any movement that threatens to upset the existing balance will increase tension. Yet there is a significant difference from the other solutions we have examined. In the case of territorial decentralization, there need be no connection with other lines of polarization, and especially not with those on the Left-Right axis. As a result, the political differences will tend to cut across other cleavages instead of reinforcing them. Of course, the centre-periphery conflict may reach such an intensity that it overshadows all other forces. Far from providing a solution, it may signal the dissolution of the state.[20]

Short of such disintegration, it does appear that measures aimed at decentralization are readily suited to accommodate the demands of substate nationalism. Whether or not the dispersion of power were based on an explicitly federal arrangement, it would have to contain the essential ingredient of federalism: constitutional protection against actions on the part of the central executive or legislature that weaken or even destroy the state/regional governments. The effect of reaching agreement on decentralization will be to ease the pressures on the legitimacy of the state, and the more diffused expression of the state may achieve more than attempts to retain a single focus of loyalty. Other benefits may also result. Although decentralization need not of itself lead to greater democratic control, the chances are that this will come about through a weakening of the central bureaucracy. A more localized bureaucracy may be more amenable to control through legislative or other supervision. However, local control is not to be equated with democratic control, and whilst "remoteness" may be overcome, the impact of state power, under whatever guise, may be just as distasteful.

Federal-type solutions are relevant to the special problems of societies that are linguistically divided or have other cultural segmentations that are expressed in a country's political geography. But do they have anything to contribute where such divisions are absent? Is there any case for carving up a unitary state even if its difficulties are seen to lie in quite different directions?

One answer is that decentralization probably has a beneficial integrative effect and that this result can be expected even where there are no sharp territorial discontents. Moreover, a federal-type system introduced in advance of demands for reform may reduce the intensity of future pressures. In line with this argument, it is better to engage in large-scale decentralization than to wait for the presentation of even more sweeping claims. That advice is difficult to follow, however, and there are serious objections to imposing a rigid scheme of decentralization. There is no certainty that the division of powers or territory will prove suitable for problems that emerge only later, yet once the allocation has been made, subsequent changes will be strongly resisted; federal structures are probably the least amenable to amendment. Furthermore, questions affecting the whole economy, or particular sectors of a national economy, may require firm direction from the centre and may call for policies that ignore territorial subdivisions. If constitutional engineering neglects such considerations, the performance of a decentralized state will create more problems than its solves.

Two patterns of decentralization are represented in Western Europe. The first corresponds to the model of linguistic/cultural fragmentation, with Switzerland serving as the chief example of how federalism can mitigate potentially divisive forces. In recent years, both Belgium and Spain have moved in the same direction in response to similar pressures, although the situation in each of the three countries has special ingredients. Switzerland presents a complex mixture of linguistic and religious elements, and its present stability is the outcome of a long process of adaptation through association, not "engineering." The Belgian case is unique because of the approximate linguistic balance and the clear territorial demarcation involved,[21] whilst for all the other countries conflicts arise from the claims of disadvantaged or oppressed minorities, typical of centre-periphery relations. That is particularly true for Spain where the demands by the Basques, and to a lesser extent the Catalans, have led to extensive measures of decentralization.[22] The Spanish model is, in fact, the most appropriate one for Western Europe to the extent that distinctive cultural identities are involved. However, unless "cultural identity" is very generously interpreted, there does not appear to be over-much scope for redrawing maps on such a basis.

It is the second pattern that may be of greater relevance: that is, decentralization as a deliberately conceived device, instituted without any strong popular demand, but still having a definite federal ingredient. That ideal seems remote from political reality. Governments are more inclined to uphold their own position and to be content with tinkering reforms to local government than to embark on a wholesale rationalization.[23] Two countries come near to the pattern of strong decentralization and fulfil the requirements of being "deliberately conceived" and set up in the absence of marked demand: Italy and West Germany. The Italian regions were provided for in the 1948 constitution of the republic, although the system of regional government was not fully implemented until 1970—an indication of the deeply rooted unwillingness of governments to cede power voluntarily. Significantly, the regions that did materialize early on were peripheral ones or those that, like the French-speaking Val d'Aosta or the German-speaking Trentino Alto-Adige, constituted a distinctive cultural identity.[24] The West German federal system, although drawing on the traditions of German federalism, was grafted on to Länder that had been largely created by the allied occupation powers prior to their incorporation in the Federal Republic by the terms of the *1949 Basic Law*. Italy and West Germany have an important characteristic in common: their constitutions were drawn up at a time following a period of sharp political discontinuity. That "advantage" is not generally available.

We can set out the conditions for a "strong" form of decentralization, which will result in a federal-type government, making relevant comparisons with Germany and Italy. The first condition is that the states/regions should receive adequate protection. That objective is realized through the constitution, and in Germany and Italy, it is further secured by the constitutional courts of the two countries. The West German system, however, adds a further form of protection by associating the Länder with a federal legislative process. Their integration is made possible by providing for the direct representation of the Länder governments in the Bundesrat. Quite apart from the question of the powers that such a second chamber might have, the West German method avoids treating states or regions as ancillary to the central government.

This emphasis gains in importance when one considers the second condition of strong decentralization, which involves the matter of state-regional competence. It may be a mistake to insist that decentralization requires a wide spread of functions to be exercised independently of the central government. It is doubtful whether a modern state can work on such a basis, especially not where the economy is affected. The alternative is to treat decentralization on a different basis: a division of responsibility rather than of function. Thus the West German model, on some counts a "weak" form of federalism, divides responsibility between the federation and the Länder in such a way that the Länder governments act as the competent agents over large areas of administration. Hence the "association" of the Länder with the federal authorities, chiefly but not exclusively through the Bundesrat, can be seen as a key feature in ensuring that the shared responsibilities are properly articulated.

The third condition follows from the second: if the state/regional units are to exercise their powers, they must have a bureaucracy equal to the task. It is too early to judge how Italian regional government is likely to fare in this respect, although it may be insufficient to rely on the infrastructure of local government for this purpose. Western Germany was much better placed since, apart from the short experience of national socialism, the bureaucracy had never been centralized, and at the present time the bulk of public service officials are recruited, trained, and serve in the individual Länder.[25] The greatest difficulty in decentralization lies in achieving a balance between central and regional bureaucracies.

The fourth and final condition relates to the financial and fiscal conditions of decentralization. If the regions are left in a position of financial dependency on the central government, then the real extent of their independence will be limited. Not only is it necessary for regions to have their own sources of revenue, there must also be a harmonization between regions, achieved "vertically" from the central government and/or "horizontally" from one region to another. The Italian regions do not properly fulfil this condition; whilst there is a considerable vertical compensation, a basic weakness is evident in that less than 10 per cent of their income stems from their own powers of raising revenue. In contrast, the West German system is highly favourable to the Länder, since they have an equal share with the federal government of the "dynamic" income and corporation taxes as well as a proportion of the "value-added" sales tax. Furthermore, legislation affecting the distribution of taxation revenue requires the consent of the Bundesrat, so that no long-term erosion is likely.[26]

These four conditions all appear to be necessary if decentralization is to be strongly based. Others may be added. For instance, it may be held that the regional units should be of a certain minimum size if they are to be viable; on the other hand, it is by no means certain what criteria are best for determining a minimum. The wide disparity in the size, population, and economic strength of the German Länder—or for that matter the Swiss cantons or Italian regions—does not seem to be an important handicap. A more significant factor may be the nature of a country's party system. Thus there is a good case for arguing that decentralization is likely to work most satisfactorily if *national* parties dominate in the regions: their overarching presence will be a better guarantee of co-ordination and sensitivity to the needs of the whole country than is the case where regional parties act as a continual brake against interregional adjustment. The benefit of a "deliberately conceived" decentralization is that the national party system will be in the driving-seat from the beginning. This integrative effect has clearly been at work in both Italy and West Germany.[27]

CONCLUSIONS

It is a far cry from grappling with broad issues of "crisis" and "legitimacy" affecting the West European state to detailing conditions of successful decentralization. Yet there are advantages in seeking a relatively low-key solution. What may be disputed in the account given here is the specification of four, and possibly five, conditions of decentralization that would provide a model for existing centralized states. At the least, it can be agreed that a fruitful line of inquiry is promised by a comparative assessment of these and other conditions.

No one would pretend that decentralization of itself offers a panacea to the problems of the contemporary state, but its relevance to the symptoms of crisis appears well founded, and it accords with the groundswell of current development.[28] As J.E.S. Hayward and R.N. Berki conclude, the principal task in Europe is to devise "new instrumentalities,"[29] and it is evident that liberal democracy has sufficient flexibility to meet the challenges as they arise. Supranationalism, corporatism, ungovernability, and decentralization taken all together constitute a frightening *mélange*; considered separately, each points to the need for a new conception of the state and its functions.

NOTES

[1] The analysis here develops themes that I examined in "The Reintegration of the State in Western Europe," in *Divided Loyalties: British Regional Assertion and European Integration*, edited by M. Kolinsky (Manchester: Manchester University Press, 1978).

[2] J. Herz, "Rise and Demise of the Territorial State," in *The Development of the Modern State*, edited by H. Lubasz (New York: Macmillan, 1964).

[3] The wider dimensions are examined in B. Mennis and K.P. Sauvant, *Emerging Forms of Transnational Community: Transnational Business Enterprises and Regional Integration* (Lexington, Mass.: D.C. Heath, 1976).

[4] G. Poggi, *The Development of the Modern State: A Sociological Introduction* (London: Hutchinson, 1978).

[5] For a review of the theory, see A. Cawson, "Pluralism, Corporatism and the Role of the State," *Government and Opposition* 13 (Spring 1978): 178−98; also, P.C. Schmitter and G. Lehmbruch, eds., *Trends Toward Corporatist Intermediation* (Beverly Hills, Calif.: Sage Publications, 1979). Lehmbruch sees the possibility of a symbiosis between representative and corporatist institutions in "liberal corporatism."

[6] In his original formulation of the catch-all party thesis, Otto Kirchheimer did concede the continuing importance of European party traditions: "The Transformation of the Western European Party Systems," in *Political Parties and Political Development*, edited by J. LaPalombara and M. Weiner (Princeton, N.J.: Princeton University Press, 1966). But there are other reasons also for disputing the trend; see S. Wolinetz, "The Transformation of Western European Party Systems Revisited," *West European Politics* (January 1979).

[7] The various traditions are examined in W. Paterson and A. Thomas, eds., *Social Democratic Parties in Western Europe* (London: Croom Helm, 1977). For a succinct critique of social democratic and other political movements, see R. Dahrendorf, *After Social Democracy* (London: Liberal Publication Department, 1980).

[8] The traditions and machinery of European bureaucracies are examined in F.F. Ridley, ed., *Government and Administration in Western Europe* (Oxford: Martin Robertson, 1979).

[9] For a recent discussion of legitimacy problems, see B. Denitch, ed., *Legitimation of Regimes: International Frameworks for Analysis* (Beverly Hills, Calif.: Sage Publications, 1979). Several contributions relate directly to the situation in Western Europe.

[10] E. Kedourie, *Nationalism* (New York: Praeger, 1961), p. 1 (emphasis added).

[11] For the 1979 election there was a voting participation of 62.2 per cent (as against an average at national elections of 85.1 per cent). A survey held after the election (taken by the European Commission) found that only 44 per cent had any clear idea of what the Parliament is or does and that only 58 per cent took a positive view of the Community. See "After the European Elections," *Government and Opposition* (Autunm 1979) (whole issue).

[12] An account of the embryonic parties is given by G. Pridham and P. Pridham, "Transnational Parties in the European Communities," in *Political Parties in the European Community,* edited by S. Henig (London: Allen and Unwin/Policy Studies Institute, 1979).

[13] See Poggi, *op. cit.* The social-eudemonic form constitutes a fourth type of legitimacy in addition to Max Weber's three categories: traditional, charismatic, and legal-rational.

[14] The most inclusive treatment of the phenomenon of "ungovernability" is W. Hennis *et al., Unregierbarkeit: Studien zu Ihrer Problematisierung* (Stuttgart: Klett-Cotta, 1979).

[15] A recent example of the process of erosion is the advice given by the miners' Yorkshire leader, Arthur Scargill, to striking steelworkers, counselling them to ignore a restraining injunction by the Court of Appeal: "They either accept the decision of three men in wigs sitting in a remote (sic!) part of London or accept the advice and instruction of their trade union. I hope they accept the advice of their trade union, come out on strike, continue to picket, and win their dispute." *The Times* (29 January 1980).

[16] R. Rose, "Ungovernability: Is There Fire Behind the Smoke?" *Political Studies* 27 (September 1979), p. 368.

[17] The British crisis has evoked considerable discussion. See R. Rose, *op. cit.*; also, P. Pulzer, "That Was the Crisis That Was," *West European Politics* (January 1979); A. King, ed., *Why Is Britain Becoming Harder to Govern?* (London: BBC Publications, 1976); T. Nairn, *The Break-Up of Britain: Crisis and Neo-Nationalism* (London: New Left Books, 1977); I. Kramnick, *Is Britain Dying? Perspectives on the Current Crisis* (Ithaca, N.Y.: Cornell University Press, 1979).

[18] See M. Anderson, "The Renaissance of Territorial Minorities in Western Europe," *West European Politics* (May 1978); also, J. Krejci, "Ethnic Problems in Europe," in *Contemporary Europe: Social Structures and Cultural Patterns*, edited by S. Giner and M.S. Archer (London: Routledge and Kegan Paul, 1978).

[19] The striking example in this connection was the career of *"Demokratisierung"* in the Federal German Republic, which began life in the mid-1960s as a movement aiming at the reform of German society, but soon became indistinguishable from the "extra-parliamentary opposition," which itself merged with the revolutionary left.

[20] Thus M. Hechter's formulation of "the periphery as an internal colony" in *Internal Colonialism* (London: Routledge and Kegan Paul, 1975).

[21] In the Belgian case, the mutual suspicion of Flemings and Walloons can be described in terms of a changing balance, first favouring the French-speaking areas but more recently the Dutch ones. However, the near parity of the two linguistic groups has led to constitutional reforms (agreed in 1971), which would give them substantial regional autonomy. The full implementation of the agreements has been hindered, however, by the difficulty of finding a formula to take account of the anomalous position of Brussels, a French-speaking enclave within Flanders.

[22] The Spanish reforms, which established limited regional autonomy, initially for the Basques and Catalans, were based on historic rights of self-government. The changes were approved by local plebiscites in 1979.

[23] The failure to make a *general* reform is evident in the case of Britain in the years following the publication of the Kilbrandon Report of 1973 (the Royal Commission on the Constitution). What resulted were piecemeal proposals for Scotland and Wales only, and the possibility of creating nine parallel English provinces was quietly discarded. Moreover, as Nevil Johnson comments, "The attempt made by the Kilbrandon Commission to present proposals for devolution without giving them any serious constitutional foundation was without sense." Nevil Johnson, *In Search of the Constitution: Reflections on State and Society in Britain* (London: Pergamon Press, 1977), p. 125.

[24] On Italy, see D. Hine, in *Government and Administration in Western Europe*, edited by F.F. Ridley (Oxford: Martin Robertson, 1979), and P. Allum, *Italy: Republic Without Government?* (London: Weidenfeld and Nicolson, 1973). A comparative study has been made by S. Tarrow, *Between Center and Periphery: Grassroots Politicians in France and Italy* (New Haven, Conn.: Yale University Press, 1977). Although not considered here, the French reforms are of some relevance; see V. Wright, "Modernizing Local Government in Britain and France," in *Decentralist Trends in Western Democracies,* edited by L.J. Sharpe (Beverly Hills, Calif.: Sage Publications, 1979).

[25] Public service employment at the federal level in West Germany (excluding railways, post, and armed forces) is about 300,000. In the Länder it is around 330,000 (excluding police, schools, and universities). In addition, there are a further 1,000,000 public service employees in local government and locally administered social insurance funds.

[26] For a brief, lucid account of the federal-Länder division of powers in taxation and other matters, see D. Southern, in *Government and Administration in Western Europe*, edited by F.F. Ridley (Oxford: Martin Robertson, 1979). The question of "structures of equalization" (vertical and horizontal) is considered comparatively in the report of an EEC Study Group, "The Role of Public Finance in European Integration," 1977. The comparison gains by including a range of both federal and unitary systems.

[27] The tight relationship of the party system and federal structure in West Germany is shown by G. Lehmbruch, "Party and Federation in Germany, a Developmental Dilemma," *Government and Opposition* 13 (Spring 1978): 151 – 77. In Italy, the PCI has been able to assert its position in regional government even though denied power at the national level, and more generally Martin Clark concludes that, "Paradoxically . . . the real importance of the Italian regions lies in the help they may give to the centripetal tendencies of the modern state and the modern economy," in *The Failure of the State*, edited by J. Cornford (London: Croom Helm, 1975), p. 73.

[28] In particular, see L.J. Sharpe, "A First Appraisal," in *Decentralist Trends in Western Democracies, op. cit.* The 'mirror image' of decentralization—hence to an extent its denial—is found at the supranational level; see B. Burrows, G. Denton, and G. Edwards, eds., *Federal Solutions to European Issues* (London: Macmillan/The Federal Trust, 1978). Lines of compatibility in the two concepts are indicated in D. Coombes *et al., European Integration, Regional Devolution and National Parliaments*, Studies in European Politics, No. 3 (London: Policy Studies Institute, 1979).

[29] J.E.S. Hayward and R.N. Berki, eds., *State and Society in Contemporary Europe* (Oxford: Martin Robertson, 1979), p. 264.

Part Two

Chapter Three

Regionalism in Europe[1]

by
Jacques Vandamme

Regionalism and supranationalism represent the two most characteristic symptoms of the difficulties encountered by the modern state in Western Europe and of the crisis it is undergoing. However, their origins are not at all similar. Regionalism stems from the nation-state's ''objective'' inability to adapt to the scale of problems it faces today. The increasingly international nature of economic activity, especially since 1945, has meant that the modern state has been in some sense superseded. The life of historical European communities and of the political bodies that they form is to a great extent determined by factors that can no longer be controlled from within the existing territorial frameworks. Thus these political bodies have lost some part of their ''autonomy.'' And in order both to regain it and to exercise greater control over the things that affect the lives of their peoples, they have to create an awareness of supranationalism and take decisions at the supranational level. In the case of Western Europe, this has been the historical endeavour of the European Communities.

The sudden growth of regionalism, on the other hand, is to be attributed to a quite different cause or, to be more precise, two quite different causes.[2] The first is the modern trend towards *functional regionalization*, whose purpose is essentially economic and social, and whose basis is the problem of regional planning, the need to distribute development evenly over the whole of the national territory within the context of overall planning for the nation's future. This form of regionalization implies that different levels of local authority will be set up by delimiting areas of an appropriate size to correspond to each level. The second has to do with the rediscovery of long forgotten or long neglected *local differences*, whose strength derives from *traditional motivations* of an ethnic, linguistic, cultural, and historical kind. Here regionalization tends to become a political demand for increased autonomy and participation, that is, for federalism.

Even though the device of election by universal suffrage ensures the political ''representation'' of the region in the national Parliament, this is not enough to guarantee real participation in the working of a modern state. It is also necessary to create a level of authority in one part of that state and to put an end to centralized systems and to central government control of local authorities.

Some specialists reject the idea that the *European and the regional dimensions* are diametrically opposed, and claim that they are in fact highly complementary.

> They are complementary in three respects. The first is with regard to their origins. The technological revolution and the economic and social transformations that go with it are behind both the creation of large politico-economic units and the present day regional movement. The second is from a strategic point of view, since the integration of the continent appears to render possible as well as necessary a certain degree of regional restructuring in Europe. This, indeed, is the logic of the Community's "regional policy." Europe and the regions are natural political allies against the feudal power of the "sovereign" nation-states in much the same way as the king and the *communes* once were. Finally, they are complementary as far as their ethic is concerned. The nation-state, which is too small to carry out certain jobs in modern industrial societies and too large to carry out others, is nowadays challenged on both fronts, while its function as the only viable political framework which reduces all that is beyond its reach to "diplomacy" and all that is within it to "administration" is strongly questioned. The centralized, sovereign nation-state is the heir to the concepts and problems of the pre-technical era, but it has been incapable of tackling the major objectives of our time, and it is this which has finally cast doubt on the legitimacy of its historical attempt to monopolize politics and to arrogate to itself all powers and rights and the allegiance of individuals and groups.[3]

When looking at the growth of "regionalism" in Europe, it is necessary to distinguish between federal and non-federal states. The federal states have been able to absorb this growth into their political structures. Tensions have occurred but they have not been acute, as the example of the Federal Republic of Germany or of Switzerland demonstrates.[4] But in almost all the other states with a unitary structure, the growth of regionalism has been the cause of tensions and conflicts. This has been the case in Great Britain, Italy, France, and Belgium. My purpose is therefore to give a brief description of an experiment in regionalization within a federal structure, that of the Federal German Republic, and then of a similar experiment within a unitary structure, that of Italy. The latter example is particularly interesting because it concerns what is also an experiment in functional regionalization. Finally, I shall consider the Belgian example and attempt to draw some conclusions from it.

REGIONALIZATION IN THE FEDERAL GERMAN REPUBLIC[5]

After 1945, West Germany was reconstructed with a federal political system that was accepted both by the allies and by the major political parties.

The main idea was to prevent a recurrence of the centralization of political and economic power as it had existed in the Nazi period. This idea was put into effect both economically and politically.

In the *economic field*, the philosophy was to be that of "soziale Marktwirtschaft." This would not mean going back to the kind of capitalism that had previously existed, but the introduction of a system of decentralized economic decision making regulated by the forces of competition. However, the concept was not that of the free market economy, since it was thought that competition would not develop spontaneously but would have to be enforced by legal means and defended as an economic principle. In this respect, it was particularly necessary to prevent monopoly integration—hence the act of 1958, which regulated competition and the introduction of further measures in 1973 to limit mergers and take-overs.

Politically, a federal regime was decided on and some commentators called it "co-operative federalism." Within the federation (*Bund*), each state (*Land*) has a constitution of its own, which sets out the system of legislative, governmental, administrative, and judicial powers.

The *Bund* has exclusive power to legislate for foreign affairs, defence, the currency and financial affairs, customs, railways, air transport, posts and telecommunications. The *Bund* and the *Länder* "compete" in matters relating to civil and criminal law, industrial and economic legislation, road traffic, and so on. In matters such as these, the *Länder* are only competent where the *Bund* has not made use of its powers. But as the *Bund* enacted appropriate legislation as early as 1949, the *Länder* have pursued their legislative activity primarily in those areas where they have exclusive competence, and these include everything not covered elsewhere: culture, education, local government, the police, and so forth. It was also laid down that the *Bund* could enact "outline" laws relating to matters such as the press, the environment, regional development, and so on.

An important element in regional power is the existence of a second chamber, the *Bundesrat*, made up of representatives of the governments of the states, which has played an increasingly large part in the passing of national laws. Another fact that must be borne in mind is that the administrative devolution granted to the *Länder* is much greater than the decentralization of legislative power. In general, the *Länder* have responsibility for enforcing all federal legislation.

Finally, where financial matters are concerned, the *Länder*'s autonomy is guaranteed by their power to levy their own taxes: income tax, company tax, capital transfer tax, beer tax, wealth tax. The federation, on the other hand, takes the proceeds from the value-added tax, customs and excise, monopoly tax, and transport tax. However, the basic law provides that the federation may, if it wishes, claim a part of the revenue from income tax for its own needs, and it also provides for devices to distribute revenue more evenly between rich and poor *Länder*.

The development of the relations between *Bund* and *Länder*, especially since 1960, is fairly typical of the problems posed by economic development in Western countries from that date onwards. What we have seen in fact has been a considerable increase in the activities of central government expressed in an increase in public expenditure on the part of both the *Bund* and the *Länder*.

In 1969, under the great CDU-CSU-SPD coalition, the government passed the famous ''Stabilitätsgesetz,'' which increased the government's economic powers. This law could only be enacted after the Constitution had been amended so as to give the federation control over the expenditure of the *Länder*. Since then, the government, for example, has been able with the *Bundesrat*'s agreement to force the *Bund* and the *Länder* to contribute 3 per cent of the yield from their taxes to a reserve fund set up to counter the effects of economic cycles.

The law sets out the aims that economic policies must pursue and establishes ''konzertierte Aktion'' in the framework of an Economic Policy Council, which makes recommendations. These recommendations now carry considerable weight in political life.

The second important reform was the 1969 *Finance Act*, which took a further step towards controlling the *Länder*. Not only did it provide for co-ordination of the medium-term planning of the activities of the *Länder*, but it also established the principle of ''common activities'' that would be undertaken by the *Bund* and the *Länder* together. This concerned the financing of investment required by modifications in regional structure. Parallel with these developments, there has also been noted a progressive transfer of legislative competence from the *Länder* to the federation and an increase in institutionalized co-operation between the federation and the *Länder*.

Finally, various constitutional amendments have gradually made it possible for the *Bund* to have access to an increased proportion of the yield from taxation.

What can be seen, therefore, is that in the Federal Republic, there has been a general trend towards the strengthening of central power since 1950, particularly as a response to the needs of overall economic policy.

This trend has become more pronounced at the same time as economic power in the private sector has become more concentrated. Indeed, this was what made it necessary, in 1973, to modify the 1958 laws regulating competition by introducing some form of control of economic concentration.

There has thus been a parallel development of the control of subordinate public authorities and private economic interests, and this is typical of the development generally encountered in the capitalist part of the advanced industrial world.

Since 1950, the need for more co-ordinated action in overall economic policy has therefore meant the strengthening of the trend towards greater centralization in West Germany. This development has gone hand in hand with the spread of economic integration, leading to the law of competition being altered, in 1973, so as to introduce some control of mergers and integration.

At the same time, federalism has increasingly been seen as a means to check central political power and to retain a number of decision-making centres.[6] The growth of ''task sharing'' between the *Bund* and the *Länder* and co-operative agreements between the *Länder* themselves must be seen in this context. However, there has never been any intention of questioning the basic structure of the federation: this has proved perfectly capable of absorbing the growth of regionalism that has, in fact, remained fairly limited in the Federal Republic.

REGIONALIZATION IN ITALY[7]

Although the Italian Constitution of January 1948 gave the regions the power to legislate for certain matters, such as agriculture and public works, it was in fact not until the law dealing with regional finances was passed in May 1970 that some form of regional devolution got under way in Italy.

There are a number of reasons for this. The first was the general political climate in the period 1948-50. This was the time of the cold war when, following the exclusion of the Communists and Socialists from government, the Christian Democrats were able to consolidate their influence in the central state. If they had conceded powers to the regions at that time, it would have amounted to them giving up their chance to strengthen their control of the whole of the political apparatus. From then on they thought it preferable to make use of the prefectorial system to exercise control over regional and local authorities, which might be in the hands of opposition parties. The Christian Democrats were further encouraged to act in this way by their need to form an alliance with the Liberals who were fierce supporters of a strong central state.

A second factor, which discouraged regionalization at this time, was the relative failure of the experimental designation of a number of regions with a special autonomous status: the Valle d'Aosta, Sicily, Sardinia, Trentino-Alto-Adige and, from 1963, Friuli-Venezia-Giulia. As early as the beginning of 1948, these regions became autonomous in a far larger number of areas than ''ordinary'' regions—local industry, commerce, education, social matters. But their autonomy did not amount to much in practice since the regional assemblies made little use of their power in these areas. Moreover, the administrative power of these regions remained extremely limited in practice, and they had very little financial independence.

These and other factors, such as the battle between local ''élites'' and recent immigrants for power in the regional assemblies, all worked against the success of regional experiments up to 1970.

But the situation was to change as soon as the law on the electoral system for regional elections was passed (17 February 1968), followed by the law on regional finances (16 May 1970). This was what enabled the experiment, provided for twenty years earlier in the Constitution, to get under way properly.

The elections to the Regional Legislative Councils took place on 7 June 1970. The results contained no surprises despite student demonstrations in 1968 and social unrest in 1969. Indeed, no strong current of popular feeling in favour of regionalism has so far been detectable from these elections. But this could change in the future because of the fact that the offices of regional ''councillor'' and of member of the national Parliament are incompatible.

The legislative activity of the regions is subjected to two forms of national control.

If a piece of regional legislation does not receive the approval of the government commissioner in the region, it is referred to the Constitutional Court for a final decision on whether it is within the Constitution, or else it is referred to the national Parliament, which decides whether it is politically ''acceptable'' (what its ''merits'' are).

Legislation may be declared unconstitutional if its effects would be felt beyond the borders of the region, if it infringes international obligations, the Constitution, or the basic principles laid down in the laws of the state. A regional law may also be declared null and void by Parliament if it is against the national interest or that of any other region.

Furthermore, the law on regional finances gives the regions only one seventh of the revenue from taxation (rates and income tax). Most of their revenue is derived from two other sources: the state makes over to the regions half the revenue raised by the road tax on vehicles registered in the region, and a ''common fund'' has also been created into which is paid a fixed proportion of the yield from certain indirect taxes that are collected by the state. This fund redistributes its resources according to a fairly complex set of criteria.

All this indicates that national control remains very strong and that where large tasks are concerned, regional finances are not sufficient to develop truly independent policies.

From the administrative point of view, the regions have obtained greater responsibility for the areas listed under Article 117 of the Constitution, namely, regional administration, local and rural police, fairs and markets, social welfare, health care and hospitals, museums and libraries, urban planning, tourism and the hotel industry, roads and public works in the region, waterways, mineral waters and spas, hunting and fishing in inland waterways, agriculture and forests, and local craft industries. The regions' activity in these areas is checked to make sure it is lawful. There is also a provision for the regions to be ''delegated'' powers by the central administration in areas other than those listed above.

As a result, there are two kinds of regional administrations, making use of two different sorts of procedures, and having applied to them two different kinds of checks by the central authorities.

The job of co-ordination falls to the government commissioner appointed to each region to act as a link between it and the central authorities. He has under him a Commission of Control whose job it is to make sure the region's administrative decisions are legal.

There should also be mentioned the creation of regional administrative tribunals in 1971. They give rulings in cases of dispute between the citizen and the regional administration or between the citizen and the regional offices of government departments. These tribunals are local branches of the Council of State.

In practice, there has not been a transfer of power in all the areas set out in Article 117 of the Constitution. When, for example, there already existed a national agency (especially for tourism, craft industry, and small businesses), that agency remained competent for the country as a whole. In addition, all the decrees relating to the transfer of power reaffirmed the state's managerial and co-ordinating role. On the other hand, in matters such as public health, the delegation of administrative tasks to the regions has often been contemplated.

Delegation of this kind is in fact part of a more general process of reform of the whole of the administrative structure of Italy in response to the needs of the economy and of Italian society for more efficient management. One aspect of this reform is the decentralization of government departments and the reorganization of ministries in Rome on a functional basis. Under these conditions it would seem accurate to say:

> Economic pressures underlying regional policy may also be reinforced by the pressure to decentralise decision-making and widen participation in government. The final establishment of twenty regional governments in Italy in 1970 came about principally in response to this latter kind of influence.[8]

ASPECTS OF REGIONALISM IN BELGIUM

In Belgium the challenging of the present structure of the state has been the major political problem of the last fifteen years. Belgium is transforming itself from a centralized, unitary state into a semi-federal state and is giving a measure of autonomy to new political entities.

Belgian regionalism is usually considered abroad as an exclusively linguistic problem arising out of the tension between Flemings and Walloons. This is a great over-simplification. The question is in fact much more complicated, and in order to understand it it will be necessary to explain briefly what happened in the past.

The Belgian state was created by a French-speaking, intellectual bourgeoisie as a unitary and centralized state with one official language (even though linguistic freedom was laid down in the Constitution). The armed forces, the judiciary, education, and the civil service, all served to spread French culture and the French language. The Flemish population, which was essentially made up of farmers and small craftsmen, was considered backward and was, in fact, excluded from power in the new state. As the years went by, this situation became intolerable for the Flemings. Thanks to a number of different influences, a movement for social and cultural advancement developed in Flanders, especially after 1870, and this gave rise to the Flemish Movement, which gradually acquired political aims ''against'' those of the French-speaking unitary state. Between the two world wars, this Movement's most noteworthy achievements were that the University of Ghent became Flemish and that, in 1932, a series of laws was passed confirming the principle of unilingualism in the regions and bilingualism in Brussels.

These achievements meant that Flanders, the part of the country with the largest population, also gradually acquired an intellectual and cultural élite, which began to occupy increasingly important, though not yet dominant, positions in public life and in public administration in Belgium.

After 1945, the language question came to a head in Brussels, the capital, where the two linguistic communities exist side by side but where French speakers are very much in the majority. There were also one or two other trouble spots along the linguistic dividing line that became ''permanent'' in 1963.

Although Brussels is the national capital, the Flemings have always found integration in the city difficult (except for work contacts in both the public services and the private sector). Furthermore, town planning policies have not encouraged people to live in the centre of the city, and there have been waves of removals towards the outskirts into ''Flemish territory.'' But the French-speaking people who moved out in this way claimed continuing linguistic advantages. New tensions were created that led to the 1963 compromise on the ''linguistic facilities'' granted to French speakers in six boroughs on the outskirts of the Brussels conurbation. Nevertheless, the tensions have not entirely disappeared, not least because of the foundation of the French Speaking Front in Brussels in 1965, since this is a political force whose demands are essentially linguistic.

By playing on the idea of a Flemish threat, especially the increasing number of Flemings and the decreasing number of French speakers employed in government departments, this political party has taken votes from all the so-called ''traditional'' political parties in every election. At the present time, its views correspond to those of not far short of 40 per cent of the people in Brussels.

The cultural divisions in the country reached a peak in 1968 when a crisis inside the University of Louvain led to a ''scission'' within the university and to the French speaking part of it being moved into Walloon territory. The crisis was caused because the Flemish community had started to make new kinds of claims for cultural autonomy.

Finally, the major traditional political parties in Belgium, the Christian Democrats, the Socialists, and the Liberals, were unable to resist the pressure of events, and in the following years they also all split into two separate and distinct wings.

These different elements indicate that the cultural aspects of the Flemish Movement are not anti-Walloon but, rather, the expression of a need for autonomy in relation to a state with centralizing tendencies in which French speakers predominate. In a later phase, this Movement began to concentrate its attacks against the capital, which was theoretically national but was in fact largely dominated by French speakers.

In the period 1965-70, economic problems began to add a new dimension to the Belgian ''problem.'' For the first hundred years of Belgium's existence, the country's main industries and major sources of revenue were to be found in Wallonia (the French speaking region) and the organizations that administered the economy, while the financial companies of the country were situated in Brussels. But since the last war, it has not been possible to halt the decline of this part of the country because of the age of its industrial machinery, the fact that the birth rate is declining and the population ageing, because the mines have been closed, and stiffer international competition has hit the traditional industries hard (steel, textiles, paper, and so on). It is also true that a climate of industrial unrest has not helped to encourage the creation of new industries. After the end of the 1960s, the economic and financial situation became increasingly favourable for Flanders with the development of the necessary infrastructure (motorways, ports, and so on), with an industrial dynamism that continued to increase, and with the arrival of new, in general medium-sized, industries whose output is high.

At the same time, Flemings began to be appointed to posts of responsibility in national economic and financial institutions. Flanders' share of the GDP rose from 44.2 per cent to 56.2 per cent between 1958 and 1977, while that of Wallonia fell from 34.2 per cent to 24.7 per cent. This situation caused discontent in the French-speaking areas, which in turn gave rise to a desire for economic autonomy in the region. Since the centralized state and the great economic and financial institutions had not been able to carry through the modernization of industry, some French speakers argued that it would be preferable to create some form of autonomous government for the Walloons. This does not exactly amount to federalism, which is always presented as an extremely drastic solution, but it does mean giving the Walloons the power to solve their own problems in their own way.

But the key question is where the money is going to come from. To what extent are the Flemings going to agree to the transfer of some of their new-found wealth, whether the state is unitary or regionalized, to a region where, very often, bureaucracy and a liking for short-term solutions to prop up outdated industries are only too evident?

The Brussels question also has an economic side to it. It is not just a matter of finding a means by which the two languages and the two cultures can exist side by side. There is also the issue of the level at which decisions affecting the economic future of the city will be taken. This in turn involves all the economic activities that are drawn to the capital, the industrial fabric of the region, not to mention the financial problems of the local authorities, the problems of unemployment, and the mobility of the labour force. The inhabitants of Brussels have made it known politically that they do not wish to be governed by the French-speaking part of the country, which has its own problems. Nor do they wish to be placed under some form of "joint" Flemish-Walloon local government.

Political circles in Brussels point to the city's special duties and tasks both as the capital of the country and as the headquarters of international organizations, and therefore claim the right to full regional status in political and institutional terms. The Flemish, however, fear that this might lead to the creation of two mainly French-speaking regions in Belgium. Hence their reluctance to entertain the idea of regional autonomy for Brussels.

Is it possible to reconcile the *cultural autonomy*, which the Flemings ask for, with the *socio-economic autonomy* that the Walloons demand, whilst at the same time respecting the role of Brussels as the national capital and recognizing that the city has its own economic and social problems? These are the issues tackled in the reform of the state that has now been going on for ten years. The present government (made up of Christian Democrats and Socialists from both linguistic groups) was formed with the intention of reaching a solution to this problem by gradual stages.

The first important stage in the reform of the state dates back to 1970.[9] The Constitution of the country was revised in order to make it possible to institute both *cultural autonomy* and the existence of *regions*. Subsequent political debate was to crystallize round this two-part reform when the time came to put its broad principles into practice.

Cultural autonomy meant the creation of *communities* (French, Dutch, and German)[10] each with its deliberative assembly that can exercise the power of prescription in the form of *decrees* that have the same legal status as laws. The cultural councils that draw them up are composed of members of the national Parliament (either the lower Chamber or the Senate). *Regionalization* meant that some social and economic matters would be dealt with by devolved assemblies and decentralized executives. The Constitution recognized the existence of three regions: Wallonia, Flanders, and Brussels.

The word "region" must be understood in the sense of an area of territory, while the term "community" must be thought of as referring rather to the population defined linguistically.

Describing the new situation, Monsieur Léo Tindemans, who had played an important part in the 1970 reform, said,

. . . the country's linguistic dualism has produced a regionalized Belgium. And in
the very near future this regionalized Belgium is going to turn into a plurinational
State. The cultural communities (Dutch, French, and German) will consciously
contribute to the building of their future within it. This is, in my view, a new phase in
our national history, and Belgium is about to become a new kind of State.[11].

The 1970 reform should somewhat reduce the feeling in each of the two
major communities that they have become less important. However, it did not
grant an equal degree of autonomy to both. From 1971 onwards, the cultural
councils were able to use decrees to settle cultural questions, pursue
international cultural co-operation, regulate the use of the language, and
control education, even though they did not have executives responsible to
them for such matters. Regionalization, on the other hand, did not take effect
immediately. Regional economic councils were created by an act passed in
July 1970, which provided for economic decentralization, but these were
only consultative bodies. The act contained, for the first time, a legal
definition of Flanders and Wallonia, but did not provide definitions and
solutions that were sufficiently clear to take proper account of Brussels.

The first Tindemans government (Social Christians and Liberals) passed
an act of Parliament on ''preliminary regionalization'' in 1974, thereby
instituting transitional regionalization until such time as the two-thirds
parliamentary majority required by the Constitution should decide on the
permanent measures to be taken under the reform begun in 1970. The idea
was to ensure that the reform became a reality. As far as political matters
were concerned, it meant a division of responsibilities in areas where
different regional policies were justified, in accordance with the Constitution. In this way, ''ministerial committees for the regions'' were set up inside
the national government and regional councils made up of senators,
independent of the consultative regional economic councils referred to
above, were given the right to examine regional affairs directly, though they
were not given prescriptive or financial powers. As far as financial questions
were concerned, a political agreement was reached to divide the financial
support of the state in the regions in accordance with the following objective
criteria: the surface area of the region, the revenue from personal taxation,
and the size of the population.

The second Tindemans government tried but failed to put through a
complete reform with the so-called Egmont Agreement, while the present
government, under the leadership of Prime Minister W. Martens and
composed of Socialists and Social Christians, and which has emerged out of a
long political crisis, has proposed (March-April 1979) overall reform in three
phases:

1. Carrying out a provisional regional reform that would be compatible with
   existing constitutional texts
2. Adding to the temporary structures and competent authorities thus created
   by revising the Constitution and passing organic laws that require an
   extraordinary majority

3. Adopting the constitutional and legal measures needed to resolve the problems posed by three things in particular: the reform of the Senate (by the creation of a Regional Assembly), the role of the provinces (decentralizing present political powers by sharing them between the state and the local authorities), the creation of a special Appeal Court (whose job would especially involve settling conflicts that might arise between national, regional, and local decisions).

The first phase consisted in the legal reform of July 1979, providing for the creation of four integrated executives within the national government to manage, respectively, the French community, the Walloon region, the Brussels region, and the Dutch region and community. It will immediately be obvious that Flanders has been treated differently from Wallonia and Brussels since the Flemish chose to combine ''regional'' with ''community'' affairs—a combination that they believe foreshadows a two-part, para-federal system, with Brussels becoming a sort of state territory. The French-speaking political parties in Brussels are for the most part opposed to this idea.

What is new in the July 1979 law is that it makes it possible for the community and regional executives to discuss matters that fall within their competence in an autonomous way.

As far as the *structure* and *competences* of the *regions* are concerned (the second phase), an agreement was reached within the government in January 1980, after the mini-crisis in December 1979, to propose a bill requiring a two-thirds majority and dealing with the following points:

1. The three regions are to be directed by a regional council and a regional executive. The regional council is made up of members of the Lower House and of the Senate who live in the region (the Brussels region includes the nineteen *communes* in the conurbation). The regional executive is composed of ministers of the national government appointed to it by the King. These ministers are responsible both to the regional council and to the national Parliament.

2. The regions' competences cover town planning and development, protection of the environment, hunting and fishing, water supplies, exploitation of natural resources, regional planning, public industries in the region, regional aspects of credit management, energy policy, economic expansion in the region, and employment. The Brussels region has more or less the same competences.

3. The regional councils govern in these matters by issuing *orders*, which can modify national laws. National legislation cannot modify a regional order, but it can suspend it for six months after promulgation.

4. Within the government, two executives have been created corresponding to the cultural councils: the Dutch-speaking community executive and the French-speaking community executive. The former is the same as the regional executive. These executives may, any time after 31 December 1982, "leave" the government if they wish.

This is the system proposed by the government. It is far from being a perfect system. A major criticism to be made of it is the way the same people serve as members of the national Parliament, of the regional council, and of the cultural council. Another criticism concerns the responsibility of the regional and community executives, which remains within the national government. Finally, the fact that regional orders and national laws are given equivalent status (apart from the right of six-month suspension) could give rise to serious conflicts of interest. If the proposed measures restore a climate of confidence between both "communities," then the negative aspects of this proposal may be considered as minor ones.[12]

CONCLUSIONS

Although the modes and forms of regionalism vary from country to country, what has been said above demonstrates that the regional phenomenon in Europe derives from a number of common causes and circumstances. One of these causes is economic, and has to do with the desire for a better geographical distribution of the benefits of economic growth. The growth of the last thirty years, which for the most part occurred without adequate planning or control, benefited some regions at the expense of others, a state of affairs that is ill-received in those regions which appear to be underprivileged in the context of the national territorial framework.

> Regional policy has become an increasingly important preoccupation of most Western European governments in the past two decades. The primary reason has been a desire to iron out severe discrepancies in economic development between different areas within the state and to promote industrial growth and employment in the backward regions.[13]

The German experience[14] clearly shows that a federal structure is particularly well suited to absorbing regional pressures that are conceived both as grass roots movements attempting to counterbalance excessive state centralism, and as a means of achieving a better spread of prosperity and economic well-being. The federal experience usually has some provision for a redistribution fund, which permits the transfer of resources from richer to poorer regions. It is therefore correct to say:

> A decentralised structure introduced in advance of active pressure serves to rob potentially disintegrative movements of a territorial nexus. The second comment is that federal systems are often uncritically regarded as a means of dividing power, but the "obverse" is also true: a sensible territorial dispersion of authority can strengthen the integrative ability of the state.[15]

As regards regional experiments that have grown up outside federal structures, it is too early to know whether anything may be learned from them.

As far as Italy is concerned, it would appear that regionalism has been an indirect means of stabilizing and rationalizing a centralized state whose efficiency is sometimes called into question.

> The regions may prove a useful innovation. They may be able to act more quickly and competently than the old centralized state administration. Above all, they provide local politicians with an opportunity to inform, influence and take part in the national economic planning process, thus (presumably) making national planning more effective. Paradoxically, therefore, the real importance of the regions lies in the help they may give to the centripetal tendencies of the modern state and of the modern economy. The familiar rhetorical declarations that the regions are "a dynamic active component of the reform of the state" have more truth in them than listeners often realise.[16]

Despite the optimism of this latter conclusion, about Italy, it seems that regional transformations are far from being a universal panacea for the solution of the problems facing the nation-states of Western Europe. It is true that the regionalist movement may partly be explained as an increasingly violent reaction against the state's need to centralize national strengths and resources[17] (under pressure, moreover, from political parties, parliaments, and governments who hope, in this way, to regain some political coherence in the face of external and internal "challenges").

> At the same time, the local and regional interests, dismayed by the lack of success of the state as a whole, become increasingly inclined to attribute it to perennial incompatibility between national interests and the affairs of the local communities. Inflamed by the new means of direct decision-making, they proceeded to make these decisions themselves regardless of and in opposition to "national policies."[18]

But it is an illusion to believe that this regional reaction can, of itself, resolve all the local problems that the nation-states are having to deal with. The development of industrial and post-industrial societies has forced states to do so many jobs and fulfil so many functions that they can no longer be sure of controlling them adequately or of carrying them through properly. The two major charges levelled at the modern nation-state are those of "inadequacy" and of "over-extension."[19] "Inadequacy" principally concerns things external to the state: the guarantee of physical security, economic autonomy, and the expression of national solidarity. "Over-extension" of the state relates to its internal development and is, essentially, linked with its function as the custodian of general well-being.

This phenomenon has already been extensively studied. However, I believe that what has not yet been looked at in any detail is the question of what kind of authority or regional organization would be capable of relieving the burden of the state so as to make it more efficient in the carrying out of the functions that, whatever the practices adopted, it cannot delegate to the regions.

It remains to be seen what the influence of the growth of regionalism will be on the *movement for European integration* and on the future structure of the European Community. What is not in dispute is that if the duty of this organization is "to promote the harmonious development of economic activity throughout the Community,"[20] then it must be provided, as it has been since 1975, with a specific instrument of regional policy. But what, as yet, has been neither established nor proved is that this regional policy will be a truly "Community" policy and not an indirect means of reinforcing or supporting the regional policies of the member states.

Moreover, European integration is bound to have important implications for the development of regional and national institutions. As D. Coombes *et al.* so pertinently remark:

> There is every reason, however, to treat European integration as having important implications for the role of national and subnational institutions that must be understood and made compatible with our standards of parliamentary democracy if the Community is to be successful according to those standards.[21]

Once again, this is an area in which research could be more actively pursued.

In any case, it would appear that for some considerable time to come, bearing in mind the recent development of the "welfare state," the European Community will develop from the basis of, and in partnership with, the nation-states.

The prospect of a Europe composed of regions that would be both a response and an antidote to the nation-state, an idea cherished by Denis de Rougemont, does not seem likely to be achieved in the near future.[22] Thus the proper road to follow is that of examining "whether in theory the European partnership could help to solve the problems of the advanced industrial countries of Western Europe,"[23] and how, in particular, the states of Europe may again achieve independence and autonomy with and through the Community.

NOTES

[1] This study was written in January and February 1980 for a seminar held in London on 21 and 22 March 1980. The discussion of regionalization in Belgium does not, therefore, take account of anything that has happened since the April 1980 crisis or the formation of the Martens government (at the beginning of May 1980), which has brought together the three great political groupings, the Christian Democrats, the Socialists, and the Liberals (with representatives of both linguistic wings in each of these groupings).

[2] J. Buchman, "Régionalisation et fédéralisme," in *Le fédéralisme en Belgique?*, pamphlet published by the Société d'études politiques et sociales, Brussels, November 1968.

[3] Buchman, *op. cit.*, p. 20.

[4] The creation of a new canton in the Jura did cause some tension, but the problem nevertheless remained confined to one small area.

[5] My main sources of documentation are James Cornford, ed., *The Failure of the State* (London: Croom Helm, 1975), especially the chapter by John Holloway, "Decentralisation of

Power in the Federal Republic of Germany''; also, *Les institutions de la République Fédérale d'Allemagne, la documentation française* (Droit constitutionnel, document d'étude no. 11, May 1978).

[6] J. Delbrück, ''From the Centralised German 'Reich' to the Autonomous Bundesländer,'' in *Europe of Regions*, a conference on regional autonomy, organized in Copenhagen in September 1978 by the Danish Institute for Information about Denmark and Cultural Co-operation with Other Nations.

[7] My main source of documentation is Cornford, *op. cit.*, especially the chapter by Martin Clark, ''Italy, Regionalism and Bureaucratic Reform.''

[8] Neil Elder, ''The Functions of the Modern State,'' in *State and Society in Contemporary Europe*, edited by J.E.S Hayward and R.N. Berki (Oxford: Martin Robertson, 1979), p. 69.

[9] The most interesting work on the whole problem of the reform of the Belgian state is R. Senelle (University of Ghent), *La réforme de l'État belge*, Ministère des Affaires étrangères, textes et documents no. 319, 1979.

[10] The German community does not have deliberate powers as do the other communities.

[11] L. Tindemans, *La Belgique régionalisée, passage de l'État-nation à l'État plurinational*, Ministère des Affaires étrangères, textes et documents nos. 286, 287, August-September 1972.

[12] The bill failed to achieve the necessary two-thirds majority when it was debated in a plenary session of the Senate at the end of March 1980, mainly because six CVP (Flemish Social-Christian Party) members defected, even though this was the Prime Minister's own party. The government therefore resigned. At the beginning of May, Monsieur W. Martens succeeded in forming a new government with, this time, members of all three large political groups: the Christian Democrats, the Socialists, and the Liberals (and drawing on both Flemish and French speakers in each group). The agreement reached provides for the setting up of regional councils in the Flemish and Walloon areas. The problem of Brussels has been temporarily shelved. The competence of these new institutions is more or less the same as was envisaged under the January 1980 agreement described above.

[13] Elder, *op. cit.*, p. 69.

[14] The same conclusions might well be drawn from a study of the situation in Switzerland.

[15] Gordon Smith, ''The Reintegration of the State in Western Europe,'' in *Divided Loyalties: British Regional Assertion and European Integration*, edited by M. Kolinsky (Manchester: Manchester University Press, 1979), p. 185. See also M. Clark, ''Italy, Regionalism and Bureaucratic Reform,'' in *The Failure of the State*, edited by J. Cornford (London: Croom Helm, 1975).

[16] Clark, *op. cit.*, p. 73.

[17] Ghita Ionescu, *Centripetal Politics, Government and the New Centres of Power* (London: Hart-Davis, MacGibbon, 1975).

[18] *Ibid.*, p. 105.

[19] Smith, *op. cit.*

[20] Article 2 of the EEC Treaty.

[21] D. Coombes *et al.*, *European Integration, Regional Devolution and National Parliaments*, Studies in European Politics, No. 3 (London: Policy Studies Institute, 1979), pp. 5-6.

[22] D. de Rougemont, *Lettre ouverte aux Européens* (Paris: Albin Michel, 1970).

[23] Ionescu, *op. cit.*, p. 144.

Chapter Four

Regionalism in Canada

by
Raymond Breton[1]

During the last decades, regions seem to have acquired increased importance in Canadian economic, political, and cultural life. This increased importance manifests itself in the organization of various kinds of activities, in demands on the central government, and in social and political rhetoric. An increase in regionalism is not necessarily a "problem" for a society, although it may represent or correspond to a change in its character. It is thus important to seek to understand regionalism and its manifestations and to try to identify the forces underlying it.

Regionalism may be part of processes the outcomes of which we usually consider desirable: processes leading to a more equitable distribution of wealth and of the means of creating wealth throughout the various parts of the society. Such processes may be disquieting as they involve expressions of discontent on the part of some segments of the society and resistance on the part of others to real or attempted redistribution. Such processes may also entail a crisis of legitimacy in the sense that the foundations of the institutional order and of the corresponding dispensation of power and wealth are questioned.

This chapter attempts to identify a few aspects of regionalism and some of the forces that generate and sustain it. The analysis will begin with a discussion of the notions of "region" and "regionalism." It will try to identify some sociologically meaningful dimension of the regional reality. This is a necessary step since the way one approaches a reality—the dimensions one sees as significant in it—determines to a large extent the subsequent search for explanations.

Once the kind of phenomena that region and regionalism represent has been discussed, an explanatory framework will be formulated and used to identify some of the events and circumstances in Canadian economic, political, and cultural life, which may account for the recent re-emergence of regionalism. Regions are always there, but they may change in their social, institutional, and ecological characteristics. Regionalism as a socio-political phenomenon may always be latent but it may become manifest from time to time. As a process whereby discontent and demands are articulated and whereby pressures for action are exerted, regionalism has in fact been a fluctuating phenomenon. Paul Fox, for example, has shown that as far as governmental powers are concerned, we are now in "a period in which power is flowing away from Ottawa towards the provinces. This is part of an alternating rhythm that has characterized the history of Canadian federalism since Confederation."[2] This trend is not restricted to governmental institutions; it manifests itself in economic, social, and cultural institutions as well. An attempt will be made, then, to identify some of the recent changes in different parts of the country that could have triggered the contemporary wave of regionalism. This part of the analysis will be carried out in relation to two kinds of regionalism that may usefully be distinguished: protest regionalism and entrepreneurial regionalism.

THE NOTIONS OF REGION AND REGIONALISM

Although the word "region" is frequently used, it is not a concept that is easy to specify analytically. There are indeed a number of meanings that can be assigned to that notion. Regions may be delimited on the basis of certain population characteristics. Such a delimitation may be relatively easy and clear when there are identifiable linguistic or cultural traits that distinguish the population of different areas. However, fairly homogeneous populations may also be divided into regions defined along other dimensions: political or administrative divisions; features of the natural environment such as mountain chains or type of terrain; historical circumstances such as sequence of settlement, previous occupation by other people, and the like. For planning purposes, regions may be delimited in terms of level of socio-economic development or the predominant type of economic activity (e.g., resource extraction, fisheries, manufacturing, agriculture). Regional boundaries may be traced for the administration of programmes or the delivery of services. Regions may also be delimited in demographic terms, such as population density.

These different criteria may all have some validity and usefulness. They may not, however, all be equally appropriate for an understanding of regionalism and its variations from one place to another or from one period of time to another. Therefore, before proceeding further with the notion of region and with the identification of its relevant components, it is necessary to specify what is meant by regionalism.

It should be noted that regionalism is sometimes used almost synonymously with region as when "growing regionalism" is used to denote the increasing importance of regions in a country. In the present analysis, regionalism is taken as a socio-psychological and political phenomenon. In its socio-psychological dimension, regionalism refers to a set of attitudes and feelings: an identification with an area; a sense of a certain distinctiveness from other areas; an attachment to a territory, its people, and institutions. It is the result of the process whereby a particular geographic space is transformed into a *social space*—that is, a space imbued with meanings and emotional connotations not attributed to other spaces.

Regionalism also has a political dimension, which does not refer to electoral, governmental, or administrative units (these are political or administrative *regions*), but to collective behaviour. More specifically, interests—economic, political, cultural—can be defined and articulated in regional terms. When the matters that become political issues are those that are perceived by the relevant actors as pertaining to a particular area, we have a manifestation of regionalism; when political conflicts concern the allocation of resources among territorial units, we have a manifestation of regionalism. Regionalism, then, is partly a frame of mind that leads to the identification of circumstances and events related to the condition of a territorial entity, and partly a process whereby these circumstances and events become political issues.

It is clear from the above conception of *regionalism* that we must adopt a view of region that is meaningful for the people involved (élite and non-élite) and not one that is necessarily useful for planners, economic and social analysts, geographers, or geologists. If we think in terms of identifications and attachments, of the definition of interests and their structuring as political issues, it seems appropriate to conceive of a region as an institutional system within which a population functions. Such an institutional system has a number of important components. One is organizational, involving elements such as a division of labour, a technology using basic materials for the production of goods and services. Another is a system of social classes with different degrees of control over the institutions and of access to the benefits they provide. An institutional system is also permeated by a culture so that socialization is necessary if individuals are to function effectively in it. Finally, there is an environmental dimension in the sense that institutions depend on resources such as space and raw materials and are constrained by environmental conditions. To a certain degree, institutional systems represent an adaptation to the possibilities offered and the costs imposed by the natural environment.

These various components are to some degree interdependent. For instance, the character of the institutions, their health and growth, depends in part on the natural environment and the resources it has to offer. Reciprocally, however, the value of the natural environment depends in part on the organizational potential (e.g., skilled manpower, technology) for its exploitation. The physical environment, whether man-made or natural, is an integral part of the institutional system so that what happens to the environment is important for the other components (culture, organization, and class structure) and vice versa.

Similarly, cultural elements are embedded in institutions: values concerning such phenomena as the environment, money, interpersonal relations, property, and authority, sets of symbols; a life-style; a language for communication; and a collective memory of significant events. These cultural elements contribute to shaping the organizations, the class structure of the region, and the character of the relationship established with the environment. These factors, in turn, contribute to determining the content of the culture.

A regionalized country is one with different, identifiable, institutional sub-systems. In other words, it is one in which the total institutional system is segmented into sub-systems, the segmentation occurring along territorial lines. Regions correspond to a *clustering* of individual and collective activities and to *discontinuities* in the interactions among individuals, groups, and organizations.

If we were to represent on a map all the events, activities, and interactions—transactions, visits, communications, conflicts, collaborations, and so on—taking place in a regionalized society, we would observe clusters of events, activities, and interactions; that is, we would observe that individuals, groups, and organizations in the geographically delimited clusters have substantially more relationships and carry out more activities among each other than with those located in other clusters. The map would reveal a number of more or less pronounced discontinuities over the territory.[3]

THE NATURE OF TERRITORIAL DISCONTINUITIES

The above considerations underscore the importance of thinking in terms of organizations and not only in terms of individuals and groups. A region is not only, indeed not primarily, a population with certain characteristics; rather, it is an institutional system rooted in an environment. It is organizational activities and interorganizational interaction that this approach emphasizes, although not to the exclusion of individual activities and interactions.[4]

Among institutional discontinuities or clustering, however, it is necessary to differentiate those occurring in the economic, political, and cultural domains. First, discontinuities may occur only in some domains. Second, each type of discontinuity has features of its own. For instance, an important distinction between the economic and political domains is that for the latter, territorial boundaries are usually defined in a formal constitution and are thus altered only through extraordinary procedures. This is usually the case even though, as constitutional disputes in Canada clearly show, there may be extensive ambiguities as to the limits of the substantive areas of jurisdiction. The clustering of economic activities, on the other hand, will tend to be determined by ecological, demographic, technological (e.g., transportation), and other related factors and may thus fluctuate from time to time, unless the political authorities intervene to establish the boundaries.

The discontinuities may also involve cultural distinctions. Some institutions are by nature cultural (church, media, education); discontinuities among them are relatively easy to identify. A cultural distinctiveness, however, may pervade institutions that are not properly cultural in terms of the prevailing language of use, and in terms of values, life-style, exercise of authority, and organizational history. If there are cultural discontinuities, it is not only that individuals are different in such things as values and language, but also that organizational rules, practices, and symbols are different. In such circumstances, an individual who wishes to move from one region to another—from one institutional sub-system to another—must go through a process of acculturation.

Discontinuities would then be such as to generate economic, political, or cultural regions. Discontinuities, however, may overlap and reinforce each other. For instance, the economic and cultural organizations that have been established in relation to a particular environment may contribute to the definition of political boundaries and the nature of the political system. It has been pointed out with regard to federalism that:

> In all developed societies there are groups striving to secure governmental actions that they perceive to be favourable to their aspirations and interests. Federal governments can be sustained only in societies which are themselves federal, that is societies where people believe that their interests in respect to a number of important matters are specific to geographical divisions of the country rather than to the country as a whole. . . . [5]

On the other hand, once established, political institutions and areas of jurisdiction may become a significant factor in the territorial arrangement of economic and cultural activities.[6]

An important point to note is that the more the discontinuities overlap, the more the people functioning in the institutional sub-systems will tend to think of themselves as a nation—that is, not as a region within a larger entity, but as a distinct entity. The corresponding socio-political expression is likely to take the form of nationalism rather than regionalism or a mixture of both. Cultural differences are not sufficient, however; a certain cultural unity within the region and the sense of common identity and of history as a people are among the other factors required for nationalism to occur. For instance, the cultural distinctiveness felt in western Canada *vis-à-vis* central Canada arising from the larger proportion of ''other ethnic groups'' may reinforce regionalism, but will not give rise to nationalism. There are several ethnic groups involved and—something important in terms of the present perspective—none can yet claim to have shaped the institutional system or segments of it with its own culture. The people of British origin are probably the only ones who could develop a sense of western nationalism, an unlikely occurrence given the lack of cultural discontinuity between their institutions and those of the rest of English Canada. Thus, identifications and the political articulations of discontents and demands take the form of regionalism. Obviously, the situation is quite different in francophone Quebec.

THE REGIONS OF CANADA

If one looks at the Canadian situation from this perspective, it appears fairly clear that the most significant regional units are the provinces. In the literature, one frequently reads of six regions (the Atlantic region, Quebec, Ontario, the Prairies, British Columbia, and the Yukon and Northwest Territories), sometimes reduced to five by grouping British Columbia and the Prairies as the West, or to four by referring to Ontario and Quebec as central Canada. It seems, however, that the configurations of ecological and institutional interests have a provincial basis, not a regional one. That is to say, there is not much of an interinstitutional system organized on a regional basis, if we mean by "regional" a group of two, three, or four provinces. There may be similarities of interest among a group of provinces and thus a basis for alliances among them in order, for instance, to put pressure on the central government. In most instances, however, the "common" pressure appears to have been an identical, but independent, reaction to a particular federal gesture rather than a concerted response.

Historically, it seems that the significant patterns of transactions—interindividual, intergroup, interinstitutional—have occurred at the level of the provinces and not of groups of provinces. This is the conclusion that Fox reaches after an analysis of the political situation during the 1960s:

> Regionalism is a concept capable of many definitions, but if one adopts the common interpretation that it implies, the grouping together of provincial areas of common purposes, there is little evidence that this has yet happened on a grand scale.[7]

One could apply this statement to the entire institutional system and not limit it to the state apparatus.

Recently, however, there seems to have been an increase of intergovernmental collaboration among groups of provinces. According to Gerry Gartner, "the modern era of formal western provincial government cooperation began in October 1965 with the first meeting of the Prairie Economic Council."[8] He mentions several interprovincial organizations formed since then involving either all four or three of the western provinces.[9] A similar phenomenon seems to occur in the Atlantic provinces.[10]

Even though supra-provincial institutions appear to be emerging and may become more elaborate in the future,[11] the important sub-systems are still the provincial ones. Because of this, this analysis uses region and province interchangeably, bearing in mind that there are, as mentioned above, important qualitative differences among the different regions.

SOURCES OF REGIONALISM

If a region can be conceived as an institutional sub-system, regionalism can be thought of as the expression of identification with and attachment to those institutions (the territory on which it is based and the culture it embodies), on the one hand, and as the process whereby the conditions of those institutions become part of the political consciousness and the object of political action, on the other.[12] Regionalism is the expression of the identification and interests associated with the institutional system in which people live. Of course, the identifications and interests may vary in magnitude or significance, largely as a function of the extent to which people's identities and socio-economic interests are tied to the character and condition of the regional institution.

Who people are, and who they feel they are, is partly shaped by the institutions in which they were raised and in which they have learned to function. Thus, some sort of continuity comes to exist between individual identities and institutional cultural characteristics. Hence the importance of symbols and symbolic behaviour: it relates to personal identities so that a praise or an affront to the institution and its symbols is a praise or an affront to the person himself or herself. Similarly, people's socio-economic condition—their careers, their aspirations for their own future and for that of their children, their power base in society—is to some degree tied to the institutions of their region, the possibilities they offer, and the growth they promise for the future.

Of course, the conditions of institutions are not of equal importance to all the groups and categories of people in the region. Élites usually have more at stake in the conditions of institutions than non-élites. When certain kinds of benefits flow to a region, there may well be conflicts among groups and classes over the distribution of these benefits. We are not assuming homogeneity of interests and identifications within a region; rather, what is argued is that a region represents a system of identification and interdependent interests in interaction with identifications and interests located in other regions. In other words, events (e.g., a policy) can occur that will affect the region qua region so that a wide array of groups and organizations are affected by them, albeit in varying degrees. Sometimes, the same event will favour certain groups (in terms of their cultural identities and/or their socio-economic interests) but disfavour others.

In order to understand the sources of regionalism, then, we have to consider what the institutional sub-system in a particular area represents for its population or segments of its population. Whether institutions are seen as objects of identification because of the values and meanings they embody or as structures for socio-economic pursuits, people will be concerned with their integrity, maintenance, and proper functioning. They will be concerned with events, decisions, and circumstances that are or could be a threat to them in either their cultural or instrumental dimensions.

Institutions, however, can also represent opportunities for cultural, economic, and political entrepreneurs and for the groups whose interests they articulate. Organizational growth and change do not occur by chance: they accrue to the advantage of certain segments of the society by strengthening their power base, expanding their career opportunities, increasing their prestige or income, or by giving greater importance to their life-style. Growth, however, depends on the mobilization and appropriate utilization of resources. Since resources are scarce, the relative position of organizations in different regions with regard to resources becomes an important consideration. There will thus be a concern with the possibilities for expanding the institutional sub-system, raising its status, and gaining recognition for its cultural attributes and life-style.

Incidentally, it should be noted that the discussion of regional disparities is frequently cast in terms of a redistribution of income and an equal provision of services across regions. This is undoubtedly important. The institutional perspectives advocated here, however, put the focus on the political, economic, and organizational means for generating wealth, cultural status, and political power. When we say that there is a concern with the opportunities offered by the institutional system of a region, we are referring to a concern for those means.

Regionalism can be seen to have its source in the factors that represent a threat to the institutions of a particular area, either as cultural entities or as systems of socio-economic opportunities. Such factors give rise to what may be called "protest" or "protectionist" regionalism. Regionalism, however, will also occur as a result of a perception on the part of a regional population or groups within it of opportunities—new or previously unnoticed—for the expansion or a more favourable restructuring of the institutional system. The regionalism arising from such possibilities can be termed "entrepreneurial" or "expansionist" regionalism.

PROTEST OR PROTECTIONIST REGIONALISM

A useful step in the identification of factors leading to protest regionalism is to examine the regionalistic criticisms that have been voiced in different parts of the country. Basically, three themes can be identified in these criticisms: (1) that the region has been exploited; (2) that there has been neglect on the part of national institutions, particularly governmental ones, which could have been expected to contribute to the strength and growth of the economic and cultural institutions of the region; and (3) that the national organizations have not only failed to participate significantly in the regional institution-building process but have wittingly or unwittingly weakened that process.

A few illustrations of each category of regionalistic criticisms will be presented. It is beyond the scope of this chapter to make a complete inventory of all the relevant behaviour of "national" organizations—federal government, banks, business corporations, labour unions, political parties, churches, and various non-profit organizations. Expressions of discontent are no doubt selective in the "facts" and events they identify as objects of concern. This should be no cause for surprise: socio-economic movements usually arise not to laud a particular situation of fact but to change it in some regard or other. There is thus a focus on "problems." Of course, countermovements may arise to preserve a situation against those who want to change it.

The exploitation argument is made in relation to different parts of the country, but perhaps most forcefully with regard to the settlement of the West. Much evidence is marshalled to support the argument that this settlement was carried out in such a way as to serve central Canadian interests:

> C.B. Macpherson . . . has aptly referred to the Prairies as an "internal colony" of Canada. High tariff barriers on manufactured goods protected eastern industrialists but forced Prairie farmers to pay inflated prices for their implements. Freight rates were arranged so as to discriminate against the West. The entire marketing infrastructure was monopolized by eastern interests who could therefore to some degree set the prices paid for wheat and beef. Credit was controlled by eastern banking houses which charged seemingly exorbitant interest rates.[13]

Not surprisingly, there was an almost complete absence of regional development policies at the federal level until fairly recently. Anthony Careless points out that active state intervention in economic development was not part of the prevailing economic theories and social ideology on which governmental policies and actions were based.[14] Assistance was provided to the less-developed provinces so that their standard of living could not be too far under the national average. But these were compensatory policies; not developmental ones. In addition to ideological factors, there were also real interests involved, interests that favoured compensation rather than development in the non-central regions of the country:

> Ontario rejected the federal government's claims that its incentives were neutral and simply confined to labour market adjustments; instead it argued that federal policies were diverting the natural and most efficient location of industry, labour, and capital. . . . While Ontario did not begrudge this flow of funds to achieve a rough equalization in Canada of tax burdens or the levelling-up of services, it did very must resent this added federal interference in the economy which it viewed as a warping of the natural economic forces and flows which had made the province so prosperous.[15]

The low level of involvement of central Canadian economic enterprises in the development of various regions is usually explained by the comparatively low levels of return that these regions offer, either because of the level of qualification of their manpower, their distance from markets, and the like. Critics, however, point out that many opportunities were missed because of lack of interest or because of a high degree of risk aversion in the Canadian business and financial élite.

The province had gone to great lengths to entice eastern Canadian capital into the speculative search for Alberta's oil in the late 1930s and 1940s, with little or no response. Risk capital was not forthcoming from the large conservative financial institutions of Bay and St. James Streets (a fact still etched into Calgary's collective memory), and the small independents were far too weak to raise the large sums needed for exploration and development. The group of Calgary businessman who eventually found oil in the Turner Valley in 1936, and went on to create Home Oil, were able to do so only after turning to the major oil companies. A government delegation had visited Britain in 1939 in an attempt to interest the admiralty in long-term access to Alberta's oil, but the war had intervened before anything came of this approach. The province was neither financially nor ideologically disposed to raising risk capital for highly speculative oil ventures—through crown companies. Thus, as Manning saw it, there was no alternative to heavy reliance on American capital.[16]

The "Sarnia incident" is also mentioned as an illustration of lack of concern on the part of central Canadian institutions for the development of other regions:

And the province (Alberta) became aware of the threat to its own plans for regional development posed by a third world-scale project, Petrosar—this one planned for Sarnia, the traditional centre of the Canadian petrochemical industry, and headed by a federal crown corporation. Petrosar would convert naphta to ethylene and consume 170,000 barrels a day of Alberta crude oil—a classic example, from Alberta's perspective, of the West's resources being used to the detriment of western regional industrial prospects.[17]

Frequently, the "low profitability" argument is accepted: the necessity of providing incentives for firms to establish themselves in a region is recognized. However, from a socio-political point of view, it could be argued that the size of the incentives that have to be provided is a measure of the lack of commitment on the part of "national organizations" to the development of the various regions.[18]

Another manifestation of the low interest in the development of a region is the tendency to use it only as a market or as a source of raw materials. When this occurs, relatively few employment opportunities are created in the region. In fact, the competition that external products entail may be such as to make it difficult for regional enterprise to continue operating. In order to control this, countries frequently try to reduce imports by adopting measures such as tariffs. This, in fact, has been a factor in the growth of multinational companies which, in order to avoid the tariffs, have established plants in the protectionist countries.[19] In Canada, regions are constitutionally forbidden to establish tariffs. But attempts to establish "informal tariffs" are made, represented by campaigns to buy commodities produced locally or priorities given to local goods and services in provincial government purchasing.[20]

A third set of regionalistic criticisms points to the slow growth or decline of particular regions or communities within regions. The underlying causes of low growth or decline may be varied and complex: technological changes, depletion of raw materials, new modes of communication, discovery of new and more cheaply exploitable resources elsewhere, direct or indirect effects of government policies or of international trade agreements, and so on. These phenomena may result in a weakening of the institutional system of a region: closing down of plants, moving of head offices to other areas, or reduction in the scale of operations. Such patterns may be the outcome of power conflicts over the location of economic and related activities. They may be the unanticipated consequences of the fact that economic actors take advantage of technological advances or of new discoveries of resources wherever these may be the most profitable. Whether it is one or the other process, however, may not matter very much as far as the emergence of expressions of regionalistic discontent is concerned.[21] Residents of a region cannot be expected to experience a weakening of their institutional system—whatever the cause—without some sort of reaction aimed at mobilizing action against the declining trend.

In short, some regions (or sub-regions) are experiencing or fear experiencing an erosion of their institutional system in various domains of activity. It is hypothesized that these trends have tended to foster a "protest" type of regionalism, that is, a socio-political reaction aimed at protection against further erosion or at the adoption of measures to reverse the declining trend.

ENTREPRENEURIAL OR EXPANSIONIST REGIONALISM

Recent decades have also witnessed entrepreneurial tendencies on the part of institutional actors in different regions. There have been several opportunities for these tendencies to actualize themselves. For instance, the new importance acquired by services in the economy has brought about a potential for institutional expansion most strikingly in the public sector, since many services are provided in substantial portion by governments (e.g., education, health care, welfare, transportation, cultural activities). In Canada, the provincial states are the main service-providers; many services fall in large part, if not exclusively, under their jurisdiction.

Resources, which are also under provincial jurisdiction, constitute another area for institution building and growth in relation to industries based or related to the extraction and/or processing of resources, government agencies, research and development organizations, and educational programmes. Because resources are based in a particular territory, they are particularly important for regional institution building. They also can generate enormous profits, which the state, under whose jurisdiction they fall, can appropriate through royalties and taxes and which can be used for growth either through private or public channels.

Certain demographic phenomena are also relevant in this context. The so-called "baby boom" that followed the Second World War had a significant impact on the age composition of the population, thus giving more importance in the society to the element usually considered the most dynamic and enterprising. The important wave of immigration may very well have had a similar effect: immigrants tend to be young and frequently quite dynamic and enterprising as their very mobility suggests. This is in addition to the fact that both the baby boom and immigration have contributed to the growth of the labour force and to the size of the clientele served by private and public organizations. The great expansion of the educational system, for example, is partly a response to the increase in population.

One of the consequences of phenomena such as these has been the growth of the state bureaucracies and especially, because of the constitutional division of powers, of provincial bureaucracies. A.C. Cairns describes their protectionist and expansionist tendencies thus:

> The ministries, departments, agencies, bureaus, and field offices to which they daily report constitute partially self-contained entities, valued for their own sake, and possessed of their own life and interests. Their minimum desire is for a steady level of activity. Typically, however, they seek to enlarge the scope of their functions. If the environment offers new opportunities for expansion in emergent problem areas they will compete with other bureaucracies for the prizes of status and growth offered by enhancement of their activity. . . . These pyramids of bureaucratic power and ambition are capped by political authorities also possessed of protectionist and expansionist tendencies. The eleven governments of the federal system endow the incumbents of political office with the primary task of defending and advancing the basic interests of crucial sectors of the provincial or national economy and society.[22]

This entrepreneurial phenomenon has been referred to as "province building."[23]

Many other factors could be mentioned,[24] but the above are sufficient to formulate the following hypothesis: the increase in the number and proportion of people desiring to and capable of taking advantage of opportunities that resulted from demographic, economic, and social changes and the fact that a substantial proportion of the growth in opportunities has occurred in provincial areas and institutions are at the source of the rise in "entrepreneurial" regionalism. The system of opportunities has expanded and has been restructured in such a way as to favour provincially based activities and organizations—hence, an increased desire to take full advantage of the new possibilities.[25]

There have been a number of manifestations of provincial entrepreneurial spirit and activity. For instance, in the area of resources,

> The provinces have become obsessed, as perhaps we all have, with the goal of rapid economic development, especially in the field of exploiting natural resources. . . . The mania is pervasive and consuming, affecting virtually all the provinces whether they are rich or poor, large or small, or predominantly French-speaking or English-speaking. . . . Almost every province has recently created a ministry for stimulating the exploitation of these resources, in whole or in part, and a number of the premiers have themselves taken on the job of being supersalesmen of their provinces' economic potential.[26]

Another has been the formation or expansion of provincial Crown corporations. Stephen Berkowitz notes "that 21 (45.7 percent) of the provincial Crown corporations operating in the West in 1975 have been incorporated since 1970."[27]

A third manifestation concerns the renegotiation of the "initial terms of trade," an expression of entrepreneurship, which strikes many as a form of ungratefulness. This occurs in particular when, after having invited or induced banks, industrial enterprises, national governments, or governments of other regions to invest, open operations, or in some way participate in the development of the region, dissatisfaction is voiced concerning their role or their very presence. This is in some ways the case of francophone Quebec in relation with its anglophone component, with Ontario, and the federal government. The Quebec language legislation, which in many ways represents new terms of exchange between francophones and anglophones, appears to many of the latter as unreasonable. ("They would be in a miserable shape if it wasn't for us!" "It's the fault of their religion and educational system, if they have not done better!") Albertans are also seen as "ungrateful" ("When they were a have-not province, *we* shared our wealth!")

The new demands are perceived as an attempt to change the rules of the game. And, in a way, it is. Indeed, both Theodore Moran[28] and John Richards and Larry Pratt,[29] who apply Moran's framework to the Prairie case, argue that the bargaining between organizations (governmental and/or private) should be looked at in its dynamic dimension. When a government wants to develop its region and lacks the means to do so (capital, technology, skilled personnel, market organization, natural resources), it may seek the assistance of external organizations (private or governmental) for the development. The initial situtation is described by Moran as follows:

> The foreign investor starts from a position of monopoly control over the capacity to create a working operation . . . —a monopoly control that only a few alternative competitors could supply at a broadly similar price. There is always a great deal of uncertainty about whether the investment can be made into a success and what the final costs of production and operation will be. The government would like to see its natural resource potential become a source of revenue and employment, but the government cannot itself supply the services needed from the foreign investor and is even less qualified than the investor to evaluate the risk and uncertainty involved.[30]

The terms of exchange are affected by the degree of uncertainty that may itself vary: it may, for example, be higher in natural resource industries than in other areas. The number of "alternative competitors" may also vary, thus affecting the power/dependence ratio and therefore the terms of exchange.[31] In short, it is a situation of "unequal exchange," the asymmetry of which can be more or less pronounced. It is a situation that favours disproportionately one of the parties:

> The conditions under which a foreign company will agree to invest must initially reflect both his monopoly control of skills and his heavy discounting for risk and uncertainty. The host government may want to get as much as possible from the new venture. But the strength of the bargaining is on the side of the foreign investor, and the terms of the initial concession are going to be heavily weighted in his favour.[32]

The negotiated arrangement can take many forms: "joint ventures between foreign companies and domestic concerns, private and/or public," hire "the skills and expertise of foreign corporations on a service contract basis, or rely exclusively on foreign investors and attempt to capture the economic rents through some mix of licencing and financial policies."[33]

The last of these involves giving up a substantial portion of the control of the enterprise and of the economic rents in exchange for development. Exchange of that nature can take place between private firms, between governments and private firms, and between governments (as when a poorer level of government exchanges some of its power for financial assistance).

Moran's hypothesis is that as the benefits of the initial arrangement start paying off—in terms of financial resources, skilled manpower, technological transfers to the region, or managerial talent—the demand to renegotiate the "contract" will begin to be felt. New regional élites and those who aspire to a share of the benefits are likely to put pressure for a renegotiated deal that would be more advantageous to them and less so to the external actors. They may argue that the natural wealth of the region should benefit primarily its inhabitants rather than foreigners; when manufacturing enterprises are involved, they may argue that a substantial portion of the profits are made by selling in the regional market and therefore these should be reinvested in the region; that the people from the region should have better career opportunities in the enterprises; and so on.

Viewed from this perspective, regionalism represents an attempt to renegotiate the terms of a previous "agreement," whether that previous "agreement" had been an explicit or an implicit one. The renegotiations may concern the various benefits that accrue from the operation of the organization (reinvestments, jobs and career lines,[34] research and development, technological innovation); on the other hand, the renegotiations may have to do with something more fundamental: the control of the organization itself; the redistribution of power.[35] This may concern arrangements between private corporations, between governments and private corporations, between levels of government in a federal structure, and between governments of countries.

THE ROLE OF "EXTERNAL FACTORS"

Certain of the criticisms made and some of the entrepreneurial manifestations suggest that regionalism consists, in substantial part, of a set of "non-market" forces[36] aimed at influencing decisions in more or less remote centres of control—decisions that are seen as affecting the conditions of the region and the strength of its institutional system. If the feeling is that those decision centres are beyond the reach of one's influence, attempts may be made to redistribute the decision-making powers themselves. This may take many forms, such as a provincial government acquiring a controlling interest in an enterprise, nationalization of the enterprise, a redistribution of governmental powers from the central to the provincial (regional) governments, and so on.

It could be argued that regionalism has to do primarily with the place of a region in this interregional system and that internal factors[37] are important only in so far as they are affected by external circumstances and have an impact on the relative position of a region. For instance, the scarcity of natural resources, a high rate of unemployment and low incomes are not likely to trigger regionalism. Socio-political movements or interest group activity may emerge to correct the situation, but these will not have a regionalistic character unless the situation is perceived as the result of external events and circumstances.

To a considerable extent, the modern enterprise is a multi-organizational entity: it has production units in several localities, regions, or nations. An important characteristic of such multi-organizational systems is that they usually involve a physical separation of the decision making (at least at the policy if not at the operational level) from the production units. The latter are dispersed across geographic areas, while control over organizational resources and their allocation is centralized in a particular location. The modern multiregional enterprise (within or across national boundaries) is a highly integrated form of organization with central direction as one of its distinguishing features. To the extent that a skewed distribution of organizational control exists, one can expect implications for the strength and growth of the institutional systems of the various regions. The existing distribution of control, however, may not remain a static phenomenon. Indeed, it is argued here that phenomena such as regionalism (and nationalism) are in many ways attempts to bring about shifts in that distribution.

The dissociation between control on the one hand and production of goods or delivery of services on the other may occur in the private, semi-public (voluntary associations, non-profit organizations) sectors as well as in the public or governmental sector. In other words, in all three sectors, a deconcentration of production or delivery functions may coexist with a centralization of control.

In the private sector, major policy decisions are made by the corporate élites on the basis of criteria, policies, and considerations that pertain to the enterprise as a whole and not necessarily to the particular locality(ies) in which it has plants. In the semi-public and public sectors, something similar takes place, except that the process is complicated by political factors such as the distribution of voters, the power of various interests groups and, in federal systems such as in Canada, the division of powers and responsibilities between levels of government. ''Political'' factors are no doubt present in the private sector as well, in the sense that decisions are not made on purely technical and market considerations; but political factors certainly predominate in the semi-public and especially in the public sector.

The private sector makes decisions concerning the location of plants, the size of investments in various areas, the location of research and development activities, the renewal of resources (e.g., reforestration), and so on. Voluntary associations and non-profit organizations make similar decisions concerning the location of their activities and services, concerning the problems to which they give priority in their programmes—problems that may have differential relevance for the various regions, the expansion or contraction of their regional offices, and other similar decisions with a regional impact.

Governments also make important decisions concerning the location of their planning centres as well as their various operational units, whether these involve service delivery, administrative functions, or research activities. Governments can devise policies aimed at encouraging the development of an entrepreneurial class. Governments can establish banks and other industrial investment institutions to foster the development of industry—and a large number of governments have done so. Governments can establish enterprises of their own. They can grant exclusive franchises to certain industries, permitting and protecting a monopoly. Governments can also subsidize industries directly from tax revenues or through tax privileges and tariffs. Governments also make decisions about transportation and communication networks, which are crucial for the location as well as the size of investments.

In other words, the policies and actions of private enterprises, semi-public organizations, and governments affect the system of opportunities and constraints within which people in the various parts of the country operate. That is to say, one's career opportunities, the benefits one obtains from the exploitation of natural resources, and thus the degree of well-being and security one enjoys are partly dependent on decisions made outside the region. This may be a matter of reality, of the way reality is perceived, or both.

What is likely to happen when such a situation prevails? Of course, if the external factors have positive effects on the regional institutions and on the flow of benefits to the region, the reaction is likely to be positive. It may consist in a greater attachment to the nation (nationalism) or to the North American community (continentalism): ''Isn't it great to be part of this country!'' ''If it were not for that company or for the federal government, our situation would not be as good as it is!'' Statements of that nature are voiced in Canada. There exists in certain segments of the population the sentiment that one's region benefits from its membership in the interregional system. If, however, the effects are negative, the fairness and legitimacy of the national or interregional system may be challenged.

ANTI-REGIONALISM

In Canada, there is not only regionalism but also anti-regionalism (just like there is not only nationalism, but anti-nationalism). It helps to understand the sources of regionalism if we consider briefly the opposition to it. The foregoing analysis is based on the idea that institutional systems exist at different "levels" and that they are interrelated in one way or another. Thus, it is meaningful, at one level, to talk of the social organization[38] of the local community and, therefore, of a system of interests rooted in that particular locality, its land and institutions, and dependent on what happens to that land and those institutions. There is also a national system of institutions as well as an international one, institutions whose activities, resource bases, and transactions transcend regional or national boundaries.

Of course, these different levels of social organization are not neatly delimited as if they existed independently of each other. The local community operates within the region that is located in a national framework, which, in turn, is involved in an international network. But in spite of these interconnections, institutional systems can be identified primarily with one or another of the various levels.

To the extent that this is the case, it would be possible to identify categories of people who, for one reason or another, have come to make their income and pursue their careers in one or another of these institutional systems and to hypothesize that those who function primarily in the local, national, or international systems would tend to be anti-regionalists whenever they perceive the strengthening of regional institutions as detrimental or potentially detrimental to those at their own level. Regionalism and anti-regionalism represent, in part, attempts on the part of social, political, or economic groups to mobilize support for the institutional level to which their careers and well-being are mostly tied.

Regionalism may not necessarily generate opposition; interests at different levels may coincide. For instance, the provincialization of a previously local educational system may be favoured by local groups and élites because it gives them access to more resources; the strengthening of the provincial educational institution results in a strengthening of the local one as well. On the other hand, if provincialization weakens the institutional power of the local élites and/or renders the institution less adapted to locally defined needs, it is likely to encounter resistance. Similar arguments could be made concerning institutions at the other levels, such as for those at the regional in relation to those at the national level.[39] In Canada today, I would hypothesize that anti-regionalism occurs among groups whose interests are primarily tied to national or international institutional systems. But this may change in the future.

The above hypothesis is not offered as a full explanation of anti-regionalism. There are other factors. In certain groups, for instance, anti-regionalism appears to be primarily ideological (as regionalism no doubt is in some circles). Richards and Pratt write:

> Impatience with provincialism and indeed with federalism itself is one of (the English-speaking left's) foremost distinguishing traits. Indeed its dominant tradition, apart from its incorrigible penchant for sectarianism, is one of unabashed centralism, expressed as the belief that only a powerful federal government armed with overriding legislative and financial powers can regulate modern industrial capitalism and set in motion the transition towards a socialist society.[40]

Moreover, there are groups that attempt to operate at several levels and try to be in a position that allows them to take advantage of opportunities at as many levels as possible:

> About all that can be concluded is that big business understands that a federal political system provides interest groups with a number of potential sources of leverage and veto points, and that capital, like perfidious Albion, has no permanent allies or enemies, only permanent interests.[41]

CONCLUSION

Regions are interorganizational systems that embody cultural values and meaning and represent arenas for the pursuit of economic, political, and cultural interests. It was argued that viewed from this perspective, the provinces are the main regional units in Canada. The interinstitutional systems are primarily organized on a provincial basis, and provinces have governments with their own organizational interests that provide mechanisms for the articulation of other interests within their territory.

Regionalism as a social and political phenomenon is the expression of the sense of a common identification and socio-economic interests: the sense that what happens to the territory, its resources, and institutions will affect all those who function in the system. Of course, some groups and social classes have more at stake than others; there are substantial inequalities in the distribution of benefits or losses. There are also variations in the cultural significance that institutions have for different sub-groups.

It was argued that regionalism is usually based on the feeling that unfavourable conditions in the region are dependent on forces and centres of power located outside the region. These external factors may threaten the cultural character of the institutional system, restrict its expression, or assign a relatively low status to it; they may also have a negative impact on the socio-economic potential of the institutional system. This does not mean that what happens to a region is unaffected by internal factors and decisions: these may be quite important and may become objects of a socio-political action, but such action will not have a regionalistic character. Regionalism is a consciousness and a political will oriented to external forces.

Regionalism may be a protest or a protectionist attempt against private, semi-public, or public policies and activities originating outside the region, which are perceived as neglecting the institutions of the region, as reducing their power, wealth, and career potential, as ignoring, degrading, or evading their cultural character, as depleting the region's resources for the primary benefit of other regions, or as sacrificing smaller and less powerful regions for the benefit of those with more votes and larger markets.

Regionalism may also be entrepreneurial or expansionist. It may seek to take advantage of new potential for growth, whether this potential pertains to natural resources, enriched human resources, cultural development, improved political organization, or industrial diversification. In order to take advantage of such potential, attempts are likely to be made to gain increased control over the necessary institutional means. Such attempts may take the form of trying to achieve greater representation in the external decision centres, to influence the decisions emanating from those centres, or to transfer control from the external centres to the region. Entrepreneurial regionalism involves pressures to renegotiate the previous terms of exchange and to change the arrangements through which regional and national or international organizations transact with each other.

Protest regionalism reflects a position of relative weakness and dependence *vis-à-vis* external centres: it seeks to claim more attention for the interests of its population and institutions. Entrepreneurial regionalism reflects a position of relative strength, a degree of independence, at least in certain respects; it seeks to increase access to the means necessary to take full advantage of the region's new potential for growth.

Regionalistic propensities are rooted in the discontinuities that exist in the societal institutional system and in the corresponding sub-sets of cultural identifications and socio-economic interests. As we have seen, these propensities can be more or less pronounced at different periods of time, depending on a variety of demographic, cultural, political, and economic events on the regional, national, or international scene. In order to manifest themselves, these propensities must be activated,[42] a process that requires an ideology, leadership, and organization. Regionalistic associations may be formed with particular objectives and supporting ideology. The presence of provincial political parties (and governments) is critical in this connection. They can articulate regional concerns and mobilize the population against external agents and for certain presumed advantages for the region. They provide an organization and a leadership that can formulate and voice the regionalistic ideology and demands.

Another aspect of the mobilization process needs to be emphasized. It was indicated that when political, economic, and cultural discontinuities in the societal system of institutions overlap, members of a region will tend to think of themselves as a nation. In such instances, as in the case among Québécois and certain native peoples, the powerful ideologies of nationalism and self-determination are available to the élites for the purposes of social animation.

NOTES

[1] I wish to thank Stanley Lieberson, Jos Lennards, Jeffrey Reitz, and Peter Meekison for comments and suggestions that were very helpful in the revision of an earlier version of this paper.

[2] Paul W. Fox, "Regionalism and Confederation," in *Regionalism in the Canadian Community, 1867-1967*, edited by Mason Wade (Toronto: University of Toronto Press, 1969), p. 28.

[3] For a synthesis and an analysis of such clustering in Canada, see David Bell and Lorne Tepperman, *The Roots of Disunity* (Toronto: McClelland and Stewart, 1979), Chapters. 5 and 6.

[4] For a more elaborate discussion, see Albert Breton and Raymond Breton, *Why Disunity? An Analysis of Linguistic and Regional Cleavages in Canada* (Montreal: The Institute for Research on Public Policy, 1980).

[5] Donald V. Smiley, *Constitutional Adaptation and Canadian Federalism Since 1945* (Ottawa: Information Canada, 1970), p. 5.

[6] On this matter, see Richard Simeon, "Regionalism and Canadian Political Institutions," *Queen's Quarterly* 82 (Winter 1975):499-511; E.R. Black and A.C. Cairns, "A Different Perspective on Canadian Federalism," *Canadian Public Administration* 19 (March 1966):27-44; A.C. Cairns, "The Governments and Societies of Canadian Federalism," *Canadian Journal of Political Science* 10 (December 1977):695-725; David Kwavnick, "Interest Group Demands and the Federal Political System: Two Canadian Case Studies," in *Pressure Group Behaviour in Canadian Politics*, edited by A. Paul Pross (Toronto: McGraw-Hill, 1975).

[7] Fox, *op. cit.*, p. 28.

[8] Gerry T. Gartner, "A Review of Cooperation Among the Western Provinces," *Canadian Public Administration* 20 (Spring 1977), p. 176.

[9] *Ibid.*, pp. 180-82.

[10] Alexander B. Campbell, Gerald A. Regan, and Richard B. Hatfield, "The Move Toward Maritime Integration and the Role of the Council of Maritime Premiers," *Canadian Public Administration* 15 (Winter 1972):591-609.

[11] Gartner notes that "shared common interests in certain areas do not always result in shared government objectives and policies in those areas" (Gartner, *op. cit.*, p. 182). In general, common interests with an economic theme seem to have been pursued by the western provinces and "that the areas of least effective cooperation and those areas in which common interests are less evident" are those that tend to revolve around issues with a "social theme," such as culture, language, education, justice, social services (*ibid.*, p. 184).

[12] These components of regionalism are similar to two of the components mentioned by Mildred Schwartz (*Politics and Territory: The Sociology of Regional Persistence in Canada* (Montreal: McGill-Queen's University Press, 1974), p. 309) as "the conditions making for regionalism":

> One set of components relates to the characteristics and conditions that separate territorial units. These are economic, political, and demographic factors, and the resultant life styles that emerge from their operation. The second component consists of states of mind, ways of viewing reality through regional frameworks . . . of a group consciousness, whereby residents express a regional identity. . . . Thirdly, regionalism is a product of behaviour. These are the political actions which . . . may be the result of conscious decisions to further the interests of one or more regions.
> . . .

[13] Robert Brym, "Regional Social Structure and Agrarian Radicalism in Canada: Alberta, Saskatchewan, and New Brunswick," *Canadian Review of Sociology and Anthropology* 15 (August 1978), p. 341.

[14] Anthony Careless, *Initiative and Response: The Adaptation of Canadian Federalism to Regional Economic Development* (Montreal: McGill-Queen's University Press, 1977).

[15] *Ibid.*, pp. 99-100.

[16] John Richards and Larry Pratt, *Prairie Capitalism: Power and Influence in the New West* (Toronto: McClelland and Stewart, 1979), pp. 83-84.

[17] *Ibid.*, p. 244.

[18] From an economic point of view, it is a measure of the degree of "unprofitability" of a particular venture under "normal" market circumstances.

[19] On this, see, for instance, Christopher Tugendhat, *The Multinationals* (London: Pelican Books, 1973).

[20] For some illustrations of the "balkanization of the Canadian market through provincial barriers to the movement of goods and services . . . ," see Geoffrey Stevens' column on an unreleased 1978 study for the Alberta government ("It Won't Go Away," *The Globe and Mail* (1 April 1980)).

[21] It may, however, matter for the nature of the solution to be adopted. The complexity of the matter is illustrated by the debate over the causes of the deterioration of the economic position of Quebec relative to Ontario (see Pierre Fréchette and the accompanying comments by T.K. Shoyama and A. Deutsch in "L'économie de la Confédération: un point de vue québécois," *Canadian Public Policy* 3 (Autumn 1977):431-48.

[22] Cairns, *op. cit.*, pp. 703-4.

[23] Larry Pratt, "The State and Province-Building: Alberta's Development Strategy," *The Canadian State: Political Economy and Political Power*, edited by Leo Panitch (Toronto: University of Toronto Press, 1977).

[24] For more documentation on such trends, see, for example, Black and Cairns, *op. cit.*; Fox, *op. cit.*; Cairns, *op. cit.*; Garth Stevenson, "Federalism and the Political Economy of the

Canadian State," in *The Canadian State: Political Economy and Political Power*, edited by L. Panitch (Toronto: University of Toronto Press, 1977); Richards and Pratt, *op. cit.*; Raymond Breton, Jeffrey Reitz, and Victor Valentine, *Cultural Boundaries and the Cohesion of Canada* (Montreal: The Institute for Research on Public Policy, 1980).

[25] Entrepreneurial regionalism can be exploitative of other regions. One's power and monopoly over certain resources may be used in what is then an "unequal exchange" with other regions. This may be so even if the rhetoric is couched in terms of past inequities and exploitation by others.

[26] Fox, *op. cit.*, pp. 24-25.

[27] Stephen Berkowitz, "Forms of State Economy and the Development of Western Canada," *Canadian Journal of Sociology* 4 (1979), p. 297. The NDP favours the use of Crown corporations to carry out government economic policy. Berkowitz, however, points out that this is not a sufficient explanation for their increase in the western provinces since, for instance, "the NDP formed the government in Saskatchewan from 1950-59, but no Crown corporations are reported for this period. In the 1960-69 period, moreover, an era of high rates of incorporation, all but one of the Crown corporations created was brought into being by a non-NDP regime" (p. 297).

[28] Theodore H. Moran, *Multinational Corporations and the Politics of Dependence* (Princeton, N.J.: Princeton University Press, 1974).

[29] Richards and Pratt, *op. cit.*

[30] Moran, *op. cit.*, p. 159.

[31] Moran discusses the bargaining parameters and processes in the case of a single industry; the situation can of course be repeated across several industrial areas in a particular region.

[32] Moran, *op. cit.*, p. 159.

[33] Richards and Pratt, *op. cit.*, p. 72. The authors mention two other strategies, but they involve "domestic" organizations only.

[34] In the light of this framework, the language legislation in Quebec can be seen as an attempt to improve the amount of career lines for a certain class of people in the region exchanged against the benefits that companies derive from their operation in the region. As is well know, many firms are refusing to renegotiate the terms of the "contract" under which they had been functioning up to then. Others seem to have begun to move to a new arrangement as far as language and career are concerned as a result of the diffuse social pressure of the 1960s; others waited for the direct pressure of the legislation, but in the end essentially agreed to make some changes in the "contract."

[35] For a more detailed discussion of the distribution of organizational control among regional and linguistic sub-societies, see Breton and Breton, *op. cit.*

[36] For a discussion of such forces, see Albert O. Hirschman, *Exit, Voice, and Loyalty: Responses to Decline in Firms, Organizations, and States* (Cambridge, Mass.: Harvard University Press, 1970). When people are dissatisfied with the quality of the performance of an organization, they may "exit" (market behaviour) or they may "voice." Hirschman is concerned with the conditions under which each type of behaviour occurs.

[37] Among internal factors are "the *quantities* (per capita) of labour, capital and natural resources allocated to the productive processes; . . . the *quality* of the factors of production, i.e., improvement in labour quality through training, education and job experience; improvements in efficiency of capital through technological change; and improvements in the resource base through new discoveries, new exploration techniques and through acquisition of new resources"; and the organization of the allocation of resources to the production process (see David A. Dodge, "Major Issues for Canadian Economic Development: A Regional Perspective," Ottawa, 1979, mimeo). There is an abundant literature pertaining to these factors and which underscores their importance.

[38] Social organization is used here in its broad sense; it includes economic, political, and cultural components.

[39] For a discussion of competition between levels of government as competition between groups with vested interests in two levels of institutions and of some of the possible consequences, see Breton *et al.*, *op. cit.*

[40] Richards and Pratt, *op. cit.*, p. 5.

[41] *Ibid.*, p. 8.

[42] On the distinction between "latent" and "manifest" interests see, for example, Ralf Dahrendorf, *Class and Class Conflict in Industrial Society* (Stanford, Calif.: Stanford University Press, 1959), p. 178.

Part Three

Chapter Five

North American Continentalism: Perspectives and Policies in Canada[1]

by
Denis Stairs

This is a large subject. As with many large subjects, it is easier to deal with what other people have said about it than it is to illuminate the problem itself. But in this case, the easier route may also be the most useful. For the character of "continentalism" in North America, like all love and most politics, is only in part a reflection of objective conditions. Its political "reality" is derived as well from the way those conditions are perceived and how they are valued. It follows that this reality varies from one observer to the next.

With these considerations in view, this chapter has been designed to focus primarily on some of the political reactions to the continental connection[2] rather than on its underlying conditions. In this context, it seeks to perform two principal functions. The first is to provide a brief review of some of the principal "schools of protest" (one hesitates to call them "schools of thought") that have emerged within Canada over the past few years in response to continentalist pressures on Canadian society and politics. Each such school of protest—perhaps "focus of anxiety" would be a better phrase—reflects a particular aspect of a general phenomenon sometimes referred to as American "penetration." Implicitly or explicitly, each also represents a particular view of what counts most as a determining force of history; it connotes, that is, a particular theory of politics. And with one exception, each suggests its own set of corrective prescriptions, its own array of remedial policies.

The second purpose of the chapter, pursued in its second part, is to examine the issue from the vantage point of the Canadian federal government. The emphasis here will be on identifying the various strategies that seem to be open to the federal authorities in responding to the problem, given the limitations imposed upon their freedom of action by the domestic and international environments within which they must ultimately function.

While this part of the book is concerned with the relationship between the state and supranational or integrative phenomena rather than with regionalisms of an internal or domestic character, regional pressures do have an important influence on the course of the Canadian continentalism debate. In particular, they impose constraints on the public acceptability of the various schools of protest, and hence limit the range of politically saleable governmental options. An attempt will be made to explore this more fully later in this chapter. Initially, however, a few preliminary caveats are in order.

The first of these comes from anticipation of the charge that in focusing on schools of protest and remedial policies, the analysis neglects the continentalist position itself. This, in effect, has been taken as given, rather than being treated as a definable school of thought in its own right. The complaint may be fair, and it is true that from time to time there have been articulate expressions within Canada of what might loosely be described as ''continentalist'' advocacies. They can be found in the aspirations of certain business interests, for example, as well as among economists who have made arguments for the removal of the remaining barriers to free Canada-United States[3] trade, and occasionally this position has received explicit support from major institutions of government.[4] As recently as March 1980, a former Progressive Conservative leader in the province of Saskatchewan announced that he was leaving his party to begin a campaign for western political amalgamation with the United States, and he was joined shortly thereafter by one of his colleagues.[5]

In general, however, continental integration—especially in its political (as opposed to its economic) manifestation—is not an objective that finds explicit advocacy in Canadian political debate, and even those who are accused by nationalist critics of harbouring continentalist tendencies almost always defend themselves by denying that the co-operative arrangements they advocate are in any way a threat to national sovereignty, or to the country's overall freedom of manoeuvre in crucial areas of public policy, either at home or abroad. There is, moreover, a sense in which the entire history of Canada—or at least of its anglophone component—can be interpreted as an attempt to sustain in North America a political alternative to that of the United States, and to do so in defiance of principles of economic rationality. Continentalism as a substantive phenomenon is thus for Canada a consequence more of impersonal forces of history than of conscious political architecture. It will therefore be treated here essentially as a contextual backdrop rather than as a politically advocated position in itself.

Secondly, and perhaps more obviously, it will be clear that the question is being treated here entirely in the Canadian, as opposed to the American, context. This decision may be somewhat less open to objection, if only because the relationship between the two countries is so highly asymmetric. The general condition of Canadian-American relations is rarely found on the agenda of American public policy debate. Occasionally a congressman will speak to the advantages of continental energy sharing, or in support of the diversion of Canadian water to the American west, or in defence of some other essentially integrative objective, and from time to time specific functional issues become subjects of sectoral attention (for example, the division of fishery jurisdictions in adjacent coastal waters, the control of pollution in the air or on the Great Lakes, the regulation of transborder broadcasting, the distribution of the costs and benefits of the Automotive Agreement, and the like). A surprisingly large number of responsible American officials, moreover, along with a handful of academic specialists, maintain more or less continuous surveillance over various aspects of the relationship. In the end, however, continentalism as a ''problem'' is a Canadian, not an American, preoccupation.

Thirdly, it should be understood that the anxieties and protests under examination in what follows are the products primarily of observers in English-speaking Canada, and they occur predominantly in Ontario. Francophone Canadians—and especially those who reside in Quebec—constitute a very special case. The intricacies of their perspectives on the problem cannot be dealt with adequately here, except to the extent that they are a general source of constraints on the development of federal policy.

It should be noted, fourthly, that such order as is imposed on the terms of the debate by the discussion that follows is to some extent artificial. The literature—to say nothing of the polemical rhetoric—that has been devoted to the Canadian-American relationship is thematically untidy, and many— perhaps most—of the contributors are neither clear nor explicit about their basic premises and assumptions. The arguments in practice tend to overlap, and the disputants have an unsettling habit of talking past one another, serenely oblivious of the fact that they are missing their targets. Partly as a consequence of this indiscipline, it is often difficult to know in particular cases whether the emphasis selected by an individual observer is essentially theoretical (chosen, that is, because he or she thinks the phenomenon under examination is genuinely the most significant and powerful of the relevant causal forces), or merely political (selected only because it is the most effective way of supporting an interest the author wishes to advance). In most cases, no doubt, it is a murky combination of the two. Presumably, however, such intriguing problems of private intellectual motivation need not detain us here.

Finally, it should be emphasized for the benefit of European readers in particular that the strength of the nationalist resistance to continentalist pressures on Canada is highly variable, and depends very heavily on economic and related circumstances. There is a sense in which Canadian nationalism is a political luxury, acquiring cyclical strength in periods of prosperity, and becoming muted in times of hardship. At the moment it is relatively quiescent. But it will recur.

SCHOOLS OF PROTEST

Within the bounds of these various limitations, it is possible to identify in the general Canadian debate over the continental connection at least five main "schools of protest." They correspond to five interlocking, but nonetheless distinguishable, types of American penetration of Canadian society. These are (1) diplomatic or, more broadly, bureaucratic (administrative) penetration; (2) economic penetration; (3) cultural penetration; (4) informational penetration; and (5) philosophical penetration. It will be convenient to consider each of them in turn.

Diplomatic Penetration

The critics who have concentrated on the notion of diplomatic, or administrative, penetration have probably caused the Canadian public service—certainly the foreign service—considerably greater anguish in the short term than have the members of any of the other four schools.[6] This is not because their observations are necessarily more telling, but because they are in large degree *ad hominem* in character, and because for a time in the late 1960s and early 1970s they seemed to be shared by the prime minister. The argument could be detected in various academic and journalistic works in the 1950s and 1960s,[7] but it reached its highest expression (or lowest, depending on one's point of view) in a book of articles published in 1968 under the title *An Independent Foreign Policy for Canada?*[8] Not all of the contributors were in agreement on the issue, but the essence of the case presented by the majority, as interpreted by the editor, was that the Canadian foreign service had been co-opted by Washington in such a way as to render it incapable of thinking like an independent representational service at all. It had come, instead, to view itself implicitly (not, of course, explicitly) as an extension of the American bureaucratic system. The argument was advanced with varying degrees of subtlety, depending on the sophistication and the expository style of the critic, but it ultimately amounted to the suggestion that when Canadian public servants negotiate with Americans, they do not deal with them as foreigners, but as colleagues presiding jointly (if lopsidedly) over a continental policy. That being so, they are quickly brought to share American perceptions and values, to treasure the amicability with which their mutual relations are conducted, and to lose their capacity to recognize a genuinely independent Canadian interest. In short, they become practising continentalists. The process, moreover, is so pervasively insidious that in the event a genuine difference of opinion does arise, the Canadians are inclined to denigrate its significance and give way, rather than risk an open conflict with their American "colleagues," which could place their friendly relationship in jeopardy.

In the late 1960s, these assertions generated in particular a debate over what was called "quiet diplomacy"—the practice, that is, whereby Canadian negotiators abroad, and especially in Washington, try to facilitate the process of compromise, and evade the constraints of public controversy, by conducting their activities in private. Such habits, it was held, had the effect of depriving them of constituency reminders of where their real duty lay, and hence led to their being co-opted by their far more numerous and powerful opposite numbers in the United States.[9] More recently, the same general proposition has been invoked on a grand scale in a book entitled *Snow Job: Canada, The United States, and Vietnam, 1954-1973,* in which a prominent Canadian journalist has advanced the case that these tactical dispositions of Ottawa's quiet diplomatists eventually resulted in their becoming accessories of the American involvement in the Vietnam War.[10]

The argument has, of course, its antithesis—namely, the view that the tactics of quiet diplomatic co-operation with the United States increase, rather than diminish, Canadian influence; give the country more room for manoeuvre at the margins of international politics rather than less; and in the end yield a greater rather than smaller capacity to protect Canada's bilateral interests in Washington.[11] One of the basic difficulties with the resulting dispute is that it has been virtually impossible to resolve it by empirical means. This is partly because historical examples can be marshalled at will to support either side, partly because the two sides do not in any case agree on what constitutes a fair test of "independent" behaviour, and partly because, even in cases of clear policy congruence, it cannot easily be established that the similarity is due only to diplomatic or organizational co-option. Such serious academic treatment of the subject as exists has been performed by Professor K.J. Holsti at the University of British Columbia, who through interviews in Ottawa and Washington has identified what he calls a North American "diplomatic culture," the basic tenets of which are shared by the pertinent sectors of the public services in both capitals.[12] Even Holsti, however, felt the need to retreat to some extent from this thesis in the wake of the August 1971 "Nixonomic" surcharge affair, which he concluded in a later study had had a shock effect on the Canadian foreign policy community.[13] But the fact remains that such social-psychological manifestations of penetrative phenomena at the bureaucratic level are extremely difficult to measure.

Organizational variables, on the other hand, are more readily visible, and in this case they do seem to offer at least circumstantial evidence in support of the basic hypothesis. The evidence extends, moreover, well beyond the foreign service to include an ever-widening range of other government departments, each of which is involved in extensive trans-governmental activity across the border. As long ago as 1969, for example, the Department of External Affairs (presumably with the help of the Treasury Board) produced some statistics on the number of official visits to the United States by Canadian Cabinet ministers, heads of agencies, and other public servants of officer rank during the previous twelve months (that is, in 1968).

Of the total of nearly 13,000, the majority originated in the Department of National Defence. If these are discounted on the ground that they reflected the rather special arrangements for co-operation in continental defence,[14] the figure still comes to an impressive 4,600.[15] The personnel involved together represented twenty-two departments and ten other federal government agencies. Interestingly, External Affairs accounted for only 82 visits and ranked in fourteenth place. Apart from National Defence, the busiest traveller of the lot was the Department of Energy, Mines and Resources, with 793 visits. Somewhat lower, but nonetheless broadly comparable, figures emerge from the travels of American officials to Canada.[16] The significance of much—perhaps most—of this activity was almost certainly routine or trivial. Some of it, moreover, may have been undertaken in defence of national autonomy rather than in defiance of it. If, for example, Peter Meekison as the representative of Alberta were to travel to Washington on Monday in support of long-term oil export agreements, it would not be surprising to see twenty federal officials departing from Ottawa on Wednesday to try to undo the damage. But even allowing for such qualifications, the figures suggest a fairly pervasive pattern of trans-governmental activity, and the possibility that it has integrative consequences, both substantively and psychologically, is obviously very real. The data, in addition, say nothing about the other pervasive forms of routine communication, including in particular the telephone. Nor do they reflect governmental interactions at the level of states and provinces, which have become sufficiently extensive to arouse the attention even of an otherwise distracted State Department, which not long ago commissioned a special study of the subject.[17]

From the point of view of the present discussion, however, the interesting features of the first school of protest, in its original form at least, are (1) that it focuses on the values and practices of the professional public service, and particularly of the foreign service, as the key variables in the determination of the continental relationship; and (2) that it implies remedial measures that are aimed directly at the civil service mandarinate. These include forcing them by political, educational, or other means to change their views; going round them by resorting to other channels for decision making and for policy implementation; improving on the processes by which their public accountability is secured; and so on. Where organizational variables are thought to be contributing factors (these may originate as ''effects'' of social-psychological forces, but once established serve to reinforce them, or vice versa), remedies based on organizational change—for example, withdrawal from bilateral institutions—may be proposed as well.[18]

These general views of the problem, it should be stressed, can be found not only in the writings of journalists and political scientists, as already discussed, but also in the works of Conservative historians like Donald Creighton (who linked the Canadian public service with betrayals of the national interest perpetrated, in his view, by a continentalist Liberal Party); in the polemics of politicians like the late John Diefenbaker (who made the same linkage and rejoiced in calling the inhabitants of External Affairs "Pearsonalities"); and in some of the administrative strategems of the Trudeau government in its early years. The details of the latter need not be considered here, except to recall that they included quite explicit attacks upon the Department of External Affairs, and incorporated attempts to enhance the degree to which the foreign service could be kept under effective political control.

Economic Penetration

Those who belong to the second of the five schools of protest—the one concerned with economic penetration—are part of a long-standing tradition in Canadian political and intellectual life, and they come in a variety of guises. With some risk of over-simplification, however, they can be divided loosely into camps on the "right" and camps on the "left." Both groups are responsive to the same underlying reality, which is the heavy influence exerted by American capital—and by American exports and imports—on Canadian economic activity. The specific figures vary to some extent with the analyst and the source, but the basic patterns are indisputably clear. Approximately one quarter of the Canadian gross national product enters into foreign trade, and of that, nearly three quarters is composed of trade with the United States (slightly less in the case of exports, and slightly more in the case of imports). Figures from Statistics Canada for 1977 indicate that foreign companies controlled 55 per cent of Canadian manufacturing enterprises, 72 per cent of the Canadian oil and gas industry, and 58 per cent of mining and smelting. As of the middle 1970s, 61 of the 102 largest corporations in the manufacturing, utilities, and resource extraction fields were subsidiaries of foreign multinational firms, the vast majority of them headquartered in the United States.[19]

The political controversies arising from these circumstances have a history dating back to the nineteenth century, and to arguments over proposals for reciprocity in Canada-United States trade. But in the period since the Second World War, the primary preoccupation has been with the role played by American investment, and there is a sense in which this round of the debate began on the "right," with Walter Gordon and his appointment as chairman of the Royal Commission on Canada's Economic Prospects from 1955 to 1958.[20] His concern with the issue carried through to his role as a nationalist minister of finance in the Pearson government from 1963 to 1965, and the appearance at his behest of the report of the Watkins Task Force on the Structure of Canadian Industry in January 1968.[21]

In the present context, however, the essential point to notice about Gordon's position, and the position of those who supported him, is that it was based ultimately on an economic argument—namely, that businesses in Canada ought on the whole to be owned and operated by Canadians rather than by foreigners (and especially, by implication, American foreigners), because only in this way could it be assured that they would function in the Canadian economic interest. There was occasional evidence of an emotive overtone to the effect that Canadians should own their enterprises for the simple sake of owning them—on grounds akin, that is, to those of "territorial imperative." But in the first instance, at least, the stakes at issue were taken to be essentially economic in character, having to do with such objectives as ensuring that Canadian firms would compete vigorously for markets abroad,[22] would undertake a reasonable measure of research and development activity within Canada,[23] provide management training and job opportunities at the highest executive levels,[24] rationalize their industrial structure in a way that would maximize their potential economies of scale,[25] pay taxes in Canada commensurate with their actual earnings there,[26] and so on. The extraterritoriality problem posed by the American *Trading with the Enemy Act* and by congressional anti-trust legislation was also frequently cited, and this clearly had political as well as economic implications.[27] Ultimately, however, Gordon simply wanted Canadian capital to replace American capital in the key sectors of the Canadian economy, believing that only in this way would Canadian economic enterprises—and, in the end, political and cultural enterprises as well—work consistently in the Canadian national interest.

There was a complementary view on the "left"—a view which held essentially that if Canada were to develop into an effective socialist society, it had first to become an economically nationalist society. Reduced to its core proposition, the argument was very simple. If the cause of social democracy were to be advanced, public authorities, rather than private capital, had to control the "commanding heights" of the Canadian economy. To accomplish this, however, the government would have to take those heights over from their present occupants—that is, from foreign investors, of whom the majority by far were organized as multinational corporations with head offices in the United States. In a traditional capitalist society, the supporters of social democracy come inevitably into conflict with an indigenous capitalist class; in an economic colony like Canada, their opposition comes instead from foreign and "imperialist" economic enterprises.

It should be emphasized that this is to state the argument in extremely crude terms, and the kind of ideological jargon the statement employs is rarely used in Canadian political debate, except among left-wing intellectuals speaking largely to themselves. It expresses, nonetheless, the essence of the "left-nationalist" position, and for a time it appeared that it would capture the New Democratic Party.[28] As it now stands, that party still subscribes to a moderately nationalist economic posture, and occasionally adopts campaign rhetoric in which incumbent governments are attacked for the assistance they give to "corporate welfare bums" and the like. The literature expressing (in varying degrees of extremity and enthusiasm) the economic nationalist argument, moreover, is very extensive,[29] and it has been buttressed on the academic side by sociological studies of the way in which the Canadian economic élite interlocks with, while remaining fundamentally subordinate to, that of the United States.[30]

From the theoretical point of view, the distinguishing feature of this particular mode of thought (in both its "left" and "right" variations) is its premise that the basic variables determining not merely the Canadian-American relationship and Canadian foreign policy, but the internal development of Canada itself, are economic in character. One of the intellectual leaders of the economic nationalism movement, moreover, has reported that he and some of his colleagues actually abandoned their original preoccupation with Canadian diplomats and the administrative élite in the late 1960s, precisely because they had come to the conclusion that the behaviour of the foreign service was the product, not of attitudes within the service itself, but of the environmental circumstances within which it functioned.[31] On this view, the structure of the Canadian economy, together with the technological character of modern economic life (and the organizational arrangements that it both generates and requires) are the environmental factors that count most and the key to explaining government behaviour (and much else). To attack the public service, therefore, was to attack the symptom, not the cause.

It is worth stressing again that the nationalist response to the economic aspects of American penetration—to the economic "realities" of continentalism—reflects two distinct sets of preoccupations. The first is with the purely economic implications of the phenomenon. These to some extent can be precisely measured, although the evidence given by economists themselves suggests that their capacity to know "for sure" can be easily exaggerated. Certainly they do not speak with one voice. The second preoccupation is with the political implications, including the creation of barriers to social democracy, an inability to conduct a seriously independent foreign policy (however this may be defined), a loss of cultural differentiation and hence of national identity, and so on. But these are linkages which, if they exist at all, are extremely difficult to establish unambiguously and to the satisfaction of the sceptical, by empirical means.

Once again, the policy implications of the position flow naturally from the variable that is identified by the theories involved as the most significant—namely, the structure and ownership of the Canadian economy. According to this view, it is these that must be radically changed, whether by government encouragement, government regulation, government take-over, or permutations of all three.

Again, too, it is important to recognize that this school of protest has its explicit (as well as implicit) antithesis. It is expressed in arguments to the effect that the free movement of trade and capital will in the long run strengthen the country's economic prosperity, and that this in turn will greatly increase, rather than inhibit, Canadian freedom of manoeuvre in other sectors of public policy (e.g., in the financial encouragement of indigenous cultural endeavours) and private behaviour.[32] Economic life is here assumed to make other forms of social activity possible, but does not by itself determine their character and substance, which come instead from other sources—habits, values, spiritual beliefs, and the like.

Cultural Penetration

The third school of protest is concerned with ''cultural'' penetration and is probably self-explanatory. Certainly it needs little elaboration. Whether one becomes exercised about the cultural dimension of continentalism depends, once more, on what one counts as intrinsically important, or as fundamentally ''causal.'' As in the economic case, however, the underlying empirical reality that gives rise to the question itself is starkly evident. Over 80 per cent of the magazines circulated in Canada and of the books sold in Canadian stores, over 90 per cent of the films, over 66 per cent of Canadian television programming (to say nothing of American channels available directly to the ever-increasing numbers of Canadians living in border areas or having access to cable television outlets and satellite transmissions), and about 50 per cent of the professors teaching in the humanities and social sciences in Canadian universities are foreign. In each case, the largest category by far is American. Even the publishing industry is foreign dominated, with more than 66 per cent of Canadian publishing houses classifiable as subsidiaries of foreign enterprises.[33] In these circumstances, if one believes that cultural communications media—low-brow, middle-brow, and high-brow alike—are crucial to the maintenance of either the sense or the reality of a distinctive national community, as well as to the generation of indigenous values and traditions and the development generally of social and political attitudes and beliefs (from which practical public policies may also flow), if one subscribes to this basic proposition, then the prevalence of these phenomena becomes the key variable in the continental problem.[34] The task, moreover, of public policy—the inhibition of foreign penetration and the cultivation, by artificial means if necessary, of indigenous alternatives— becomes obvious. And once again there is a vast literature on the subject,[35] together with a relatively impressive array of government responses. The latter will be discussed further below.

Informational Penetration

The origins of the fourth school of protest, preoccupied with the problem of informational penetration, is similarly self-evident, and while it can be argued that it has very great significance for the conduct of Canadian external affairs in general and Canadian-American relations in particular, it probably requires no more than cursory elaboration. The basic concern here is with the fact that so much of the information upon which Canadians base their responses to world affairs and their assessments of Canadian government policies abroad comes directly from foreign, and particularly from American, news sources. This is partly a side-effect of the patterns of magazine circulation and television coverage already mentioned. More directly, however, it results from the massive dependence of both the print and electronic media on external sources of international news, a phenomenon that has been thoroughly documented in both private studies and government reports.[36] These external sources include the major wire services, like AP, Reuter, A-F P, and UPI, as well as the syndicated services of major foreign dailies (notably the *New York Times, Washington Post,* and *Le Monde*) and weeklies (like the *Observer*). They also include video tape from CBS and other foreign television networks, which are heavily tapped by the producers of Canadian television news programmes. Even the newspaper copy distributed by the Canadian Press co-operative news agency, when date-lined abroad, is almost always composed of reslugged (occasionally rewritten) material from AP or Reuter wires.[37]

For good and obvious reasons, those who are preoccupied with this problem normally do not assign to it the all-encompassing importance attributed, for example, to the economic variable by economic nationalists.[38] Nonetheless, depending on one's conception of the ''news,'' and of the role it plays in determining the domestic perceptions and ultimately the politics upon which foreign policy decisions are at least partly founded, it can be regarded as an extremely significant mechanism of American penetration. It can also be viewed as an important source of reinforcement for penetrations of other kinds—economic and cultural, for example. In this case, the policy implications are less clear—at least in the context of Canadian views about the freedom and independence of the press—since the prospect of government intervention, even in the form of offers of financial support, raises at once the spectre of government-controlled media.[39] Such pressures for change as exist, therefore, tend to be directed to the publishers, editors, and broadcast managers who ultimately control the news-processing system. Since these pressures in practice are relatively weak and intermittent, and since they are not accompanied by credible threats of sanctions for failure to comply, they have not yet produced visible results.

Philosophical Penetration

The last school of protest, arising in response to what may be described as ''philosophical'' penetration, is unlike the others in that it does not really lend itself, even in hypothetical terms, to practical remedies. This is essentially because it approaches the problem at a much more fundamental level, and is rooted in the view that ''ideas''—in the sense of basic ideas about the nature of knowledge, the foundations of ethics, and the organization of the ideal society—are ultimately the real source of political and social behaviour. Certainly, on this view, they are more profoundly significant as causal factors than are the forces of economics, which are taken themselves to be the product of ideas, rather than, as Marx would have it, the other way round. The most visible spokesman for this position in Canada is George Grant, who has argued in essence that any prospect of a distinct (and especially a conservatively distinct) Canadian society and polity has disappeared as a result of the dissemination of American (originally British) political, economic, and epistemological beliefs dating most obviously to the eighteenth century—that is, to the American revolution—but originating ultimately in the religious and scientific transformations of post-medieval Europe. The power of the American variant of the liberal idea, he argues, when coupled with the growth of technology and certain fundamental notions of progress, has been so great that it has completely undermined any possibility of an alternative conception of the ''good society'' in Canada, and in varying degrees in most other parts of the Western world as well. Canada's *de facto*, if not yet *de jure*, absorption into the American Empire is the unavoidable consequence. No practical action can be taken, moreover, to correct the problem. This is partly because it is in the nature of the beast that it is not generally perceived as a ''problem'' at all, and partly because the difficulty could not be overcome without the same sort of massive transformation of intellectual assumptions as occurred in Europe after the Middle Ages. Before the root premises of the societies over which they preside, even the most authoritarian of governments, on this view, are essentially helpless. Such traces of the organic conception of community, as softened and moderated the liberal idea among the Empire Loyalists of English-speaking Canada, and in the traditional Roman Catholic communities of Acadia and Quebec,[40] have thus perished before the onslaught of the American example. Hence the melancholy title of Grant's political tract: *Lament for a Nation.*[41]

The parallelist monotony of the foregoing exposition may be thought unnecessarily trying. It seems useful, nonetheless, to stress again the linkages between the various schools of protest on the one hand, and their respective theoretical premises and consequent policy implications on the other. Whether in particular cases the political advocacies came first and the supporting analysis, second, or the other way round, remains an open question. Presumably the answer would vary from one disputant to the next. But that the linkages do exist at the analytical level appears beyond doubt.

It should be emphasized once more, as well, that the classification of the five lines of argument reflects the way in which the problem has been examined in the context of political debate by attentive publics. From the point of view of academic political science, the notion that there can be a single-variable explanation of so complex a relationship must be regarded with considerable suspicion. It can be argued in any event that it is the practical effect of all the various forms of penetration taken together that is significant. One of the reasons for the severity of the problem in Canada (relatively to countries in the Third World, and in other areas where similar anxieties are expressed) is that in the Canadian case, the forces involved are so obviously interlocked and mutually supportive,[42] strengthened as they are by geographical proximity and by a commonality of language (francophones apart) with that of the penetrating polity. They are enhanced, too, by the absence in Canadian history of such dramatic experiences (revolutions, for example, or conquests) as are the source in other societies of distinctive nation-building mythologies.[43]

Academic social scientists have attempted, from time to time, to come to grips in a more detached way with this problem of synthesis, and in at least a few cases their efforts have involved the application of more or less systematic analytical frameworks. Among the most promising has been that of integration theory. This draws, of course, on the basic notion that if two or more separate political communities come to interact with one another in a sufficient number of functional fields, and in sufficient degree, they will move in fact, if not at first formally in law, towards the creation of a single polity.[44] The conclusions of analysts who have tested this thesis against the Canadian-American example have not been in agreement, however, and at least one of them has argued that as the evidence of functional integration becomes more obvious, it sparks a hostile reaction in the weaker power, which reverses the progress towards a matching integration at the political or constitutional level. More specifically, where only two powers are involved, and where their respective capabilities are very uneven, a kind of self-regulator, or governor, operates through feedback mechanisms in the smaller actor to inhibit the integrative process.[45]

The interpretive difficulties here have been complicated further by the fact that different observers have held different views of what an "integrated" community would actually look like, and hence have applied different tests to the evidence (which is in any case sufficiently varied and complex to accommodate almost any point of view). What appears to one analyst as an integrated "continental community" is thus perceived by another as a diplomatic battlefield.

One of the results of these confusions has been a tendency to disaggregate the phenomenon again, and to identify different *kinds* of "integration."[46] This obviously makes the problem of developing specific measures or indicators for the various integrative processes thus defined much easier, but it also begs the ultimate question, and brings the debate back full circle to where it began (albeit with improved quality of evidence and greater analytical precision).

A second framework that has been applied to the Canada-United States relationship can be described as "transnational analysis." In its current manifestation, the perspective was first developed by two American scholars, Joseph Nye and Robert Keohane, and was originally intended as a framework for the study of international politics at large.[47] In contrast with integration theory, it seeks essentially to show that non-governmental, or sub-governmental, interactions between national communities lead not so much to the amalgamation of governments as to their demotion. On this view, the substance of intergovernmental behaviour is really determined by the environments within which government decision makers function. These environments are held, in turn, to be shaped in large degree by the transnational activities of non-governmental (and transgovernmental[48]) actors. It follows from this premise that the tradition of studying relations between countries almost entirely in terms of the interactions of the governments involved distorts—certainly it neglects—many of the most important processes of international politics. In circumstances in which two or more polities have extensive exchanges at non-governmental levels, therefore, the governments themselves act more as mirrors of these other conditions than as initiators of behaviour in their own right. Even very large disparities in state ''power'' as traditionally conceived may not then be particularly significant.

An ambitious attempt to apply the transnational framework to the Canadian-American relationship was subsequently undertaken by a team of specialists drawn from both sides of the border, the results of which were published in the autumn 1974 issue of *International Organization*.[49] Some excellent case-studies emerged, and the increasing prevalence of transnational relationships between the two countries was clearly documented. At the crude level of intergovernmental bargaining, moreover, it became clear that—penetrated or not—Ottawa does not always ''lose'' in its negotiating engagements with Washington. Again, however, the disaggregated character of the individual studies, and the variability of the patterns from one context to the next, made it difficult for the editors to draw firm conclusions about the implications of transnational activity for the development of the continental relationship as a whole.[50]

Other synthesizing frameworks are obviously available—systems analysis, for example, or various derivatives of Marxism[51]—and some students of the subject have made the vocabulary of power (using concepts like ''dominance,'' or ''Finlandization,'' or the notion of an ''asymmetric dyad'') central to their analyses.[52] After the fashion of Johan Galtung, there are quarrels, too, over whether the relationship can best be described as ''interdependent'' or ''dependent.'' Partly because of the absence of reliable and shared empirical referents, however, there has been little agreement on what test of evidence should be applied, and thus far none of these approaches has acquired the status of a conventional wisdom. The analytical problems they pose tend, in any case, to lead the discussion away from the domain of common political debate, which is the primary focus of the present chapter. It is time, therefore, to shift gears, and examine the issue as a dilemma of Canadian government.

POLICY RESPONSES

It is at the governmental level that the constraints arising from regional (and other) diversities within Canada begin to enter the equation as inhibiting elements. This is partly because the various forms of penetration are not perceived in the same way, or as having the same significance, in different parts of the country. It is also because the costs and benefits or the proposed policy remedies fall very unevenly from one region to the next. The constituency pressure in support of the various schools of protest is thus not homogeneously distributed. The anxieties of particular regions, moreover, often find powerful political expression through the actions of provincial governments, to say nothing of pressure groups, the rank-and-file members of political parties, the mass media, and other domestic sources of governmental inconvenience. From the policy maker's point of view, as well, there are complications arising from the countervailing pressures of the United States itself—pressures that can be very severe, and that are often anticipated in the policy-making process even where they have not yet been formally expressed. The range of acceptable options is limited, too, by constraints deriving from fundamental conceptions of what constitute the limits of legitimate government intervention in the economy and in society at large.

Taking these factors into account, it would appear that Canadian governments have at their disposal five basic strategies for dealing with the problem of "continental pull."[53] They may be described as "counter-integrative techniques." Each of them suffers from its own political and other limitations, and within the range of realistic choices, none of them by itself offers a clear, much less a permanent, solution. At the most general level, therefore, the character of any particular federal government's "policy" in this area is defined, not by its selection of one strategy over the others, but by the way in which it consciously or unconsciously mixes them together.[54] With the help of some lamentably graceless jargon, the five possibilities may be identified as (1) diversification, (2) multilateralization, (3) fragmentation, (4) substitution (or nation building), and (5) disengagement (or roll-back).[55] Each of them can be considered in turn.

Strategies of Diversification

These seek to diminish the impact of the United States on Canadian life, not by attacking the Canadian-American relationship directly, but by attempting to develop additional (and countervailing) linkages with other foreign powers. The traditional targets have been Britain (together with parts of the Commonwealth) and Western Europe. Among the developed countries, Japan has recently been added to the list and will doubtless grow in importance. With varying degrees of optimism, some of the developing countries have also been viewed as potential long-term targets of opportunity, and wistful mention has sometimes been made of the special case represented by the larger powers of Latin America.

The diversification strategy is *prima facie* an attractive one, and in broad outline is likely to remain a permanent feature of Canadian foreign policy. At the same time, it suffers from at least three main disadvantages or uncertainties. The first is that it ultimately relies for its success on the active support of private organizations and individuals, and hence is not fully under the administrative control of the government. Public policy initiatives can seek to make opportunities available, can attempt to ensure that Canadians are aware of them, and through tax incentives and the like can try to make them appear more attractive. In the final analysis, however, a great deal must be left to the private sector, which may not be very responsive.

The second limitation of the strategy is that it also depends on the willing co-operation of third parties—that is, the governments and the relevant constituencies of the targeted states. Such co-operation, as in the case of the so-called ''contractual link'' between Canada and the European Community, is sometimes easier to secure in principle than it is in practice.

The third limitation is unlike the other two in that it relates not to problems of implementation, but to results. In particular, it is not clear that even a successful diversification strategy actually serves in every case to countervail American influence. It is even conceivable that in some fields it could diminish, rather than expand, the government's real freedom of manoeuvre. There is nothing automatic, after all, in the proposition that a mouse is safer in bed with three elephants than one, even if he can play off the twitches of the heaviest against the grunts of the other two.

Strategies of Multilateralization

These strategies are ultimately aimed at diluting the American impact on Canadian policy by forcing as many as possible of the amenable items on the international agenda into multilateral decision-making contexts. The issues involved then become subject to a variety of cross-pressuring influences, and the difficulties of dealing bilaterally with a much greater power are muted. This, too, has been a fairly persistent characteristic of Canadian policy, and provides at least part of the rationale for Ottawa's active support of such organizations as the United Nations and the North Atlantic alliance, and for its periodic attempts to broaden the scope of their respective spheres of activity. The pattern has been especially noticeable in the context of politico-security issues arising from the cold war, but there are examples in ''functional'' areas of foreign policy as well. Perhaps the most spectacular of the recent illustrations is provided by the aggressive Canadian role in conferences on the law of the sea.

These strategies, however, have a number of obvious deficiencies, of which three are particularly important. The first is that not all the relevant issues are amenable to the multilateral approach, and some observers would go so far as to argue that many of the excluded items are in fact the most important (for example, those bearing on foreign investment, resource extraction, or cultural penetration). The second is that multilateral organizations do not always operate in the Canadian interest, and it is even possible to make the case that on a broad range of contentious international problems, the much-enlarged United Nations has actually become an inhospitable environment for the conduct of Canadian diplomacy. Even where this is not so, resort to a multilateral forum enormously complicates the political forces involved, and makes accurate predictions of outcomes much more difficult. The third deficiency is even more obvious, for the United States (in this case) may not be prepared to play the multilateral game, especially if it perceives a clear and overriding threat to its interests in so doing. The multilateralist strategy thus has limited capabilities and cannot be regarded as a panacea.

Fragmentation Strategies

These amount to a kind of "planned ad hocery," by which every effort is made to deal with Washington on an "issue-by-issue" basis, rather than linking issues together and aiming for package deals. The assumption is that if disputes are approached on a "rational" or "problem-solving" basis, the chances of their being resolved on their merits, instead of on the basis of bargaining power alone (where the Americans have a natural advantage), are greatly enhanced. The risk of escalation, and hence of inconveniently emotional intrusions by the general public, is in this way also reduced to a minimum on both sides of the border.

This strategy, too, has been a relatively persistent feature of Canadian diplomatic practice, and with occasional exceptions it has been reciprocated on the American side. It does carry with it the danger that Canadian negotiators will be co-opted into compromising more readily than they should, and into viewing issues in continental rather than national terms. It raises, that is, the problem of quiet diplomacy and diplomatic penetration discussed earlier. It also accentuates the federal government's "management" problem, in the sense that it makes co-ordination of the relationship as a whole administratively more difficult.[56] Its principal limitation, however, derives from its reliance on the level of conflict being relatively low, even in disputed cases—a condition that is possible only because the items involved normally matter much less to the United States than to Canada. The accommodative processes required can break down in the event that particular disputes develop a high level of public visibility, or a significant degree of substantive importance, on the American side of the border. The prudent disposition of most Canadian governments has been to give way before this happens, but such anticipatory retreats may not always be possible.[57]

Substitution, or "Nation-Building," Strategies

Such strategies are both familiar and self-explanatory. They seek to diminish the impact of American pressures on Canadian life, not by attacking the pressures themselves, but by creating indigenous alternatives within Canada. Such strategies have a long and prominent place in Canadian history, and are reflected in a variety of government initiatives beginning (at least) with the "national policy" of Sir John A. Macdonald in the confederation period, and extending in later decades to such measures as the creation of the Canadian Broadcasting Corporation, the establishment of the National Film Board, the founding of the Canada Council, the construction of the Trans-Canada Highway, the formation of the Canadian Radio-Television Commission, the provision of subsidies for Canadian book publishers, and a variety of others.

The strategy has a number of obvious advantages. Except in the case of subsidies to economic enterprises, which have an export capability in competition with firms in the United States, the policies involved can be pursued without arousing irritations in Washington or elsewhere. Although they naturally attract supportive constituencies once they are in place, they are nonetheless subject, within certain broad limits, to amendment by governing authorities. In that sense, they are managerially efficient instruments of public policy. Their substance, moreover, is inherently constructive, which makes it possible for them to contribute in a positive way to the richness and variety of national life. Because the strategy can be instituted without impinging directly on the free flow of ideas from abroad, and therefore without challenging fundamental values relating to freedom of thought and expression, it is a particularly attractive option in the cultural field.

On the debit side, there is a minor disadvantage in that cultural activities of all kinds are prone to heated debate, and the policies that give rise to them are therefore subject to controversy (as any CBC executive will testify). There is also a more serious problem in that such policies often have the effect of stimulating the centre of the country (where the "critical mass" of cultural labour is located) at the expense of the peripheral regions, which may in consequence become angry and resentful. Most such disputes are containable, however, and ultimately the strategy's principal limitation is its cost, apart from the restrictions imposed by the general view that there are certain activities in which governments ought not to be involved. Nonetheless, the nation-building approach, more than the others on the list, has in many fields a creative capacity that can be very attractive to political leaderships anxious to leave visible traces of their time in office.

Disengagement, or Roll-Back, Strategies

These are politically the most difficult to implement. They consist in attemps to deal with specific forms of American penetration by attacking them directly. The limitations of the roll-back approach arise from the fact that once a particular relationship has been established, it creates its own ''dependents''—those who receive benefits from it—on both sides of the border, and these are naturally prone to defending their interests. Initiatives on the part of the government to dismantle the arrangements involved are therefore often met with intense opposition in both Canada and the United States. The result is that such measures are deployed only on rare occasions, and even then at the risk of considerable controversy. The heated debate generated by the removal of tax benefits for businesses advertising in *Time* and *Reader's Digest* provides a concrete example,[58] as does the vigorous American reaction to the recent Saskatchewan initiatives in the potash industry. The failure of nationalist proposals to promote ''buy-back'' policies in relation to subsidiaries of American corporations operating in key sectors of the Canadian economy also illustrates the strength of the political forces involved.

In these circumstances, the tendency is to fall back to a defensive posture—to act, that is, in such a way as to prevent further growth rather than to disengage from existing linkages. This pattern has been particularly obvious in the field of banking, where it has been hotly contested by the American interests involved but has succeeded in the end largely because governing authorities on both sides of the border agree that the regulation of banking institutions, like the control of armies, is a natural and necessary function of the sovereign state. The Foreign Investment Review Agency established by the Trudeau government also provides a classic example of this sort of defensive ''gatekeeping,'' and the political controversies it has generated—in spite of its ginger approach to the performance of its responsibilities—illustrate again the practical limitations of even relatively weak forms of the roll-back approach.

It is tempting, perhaps, to add a sixth strategy to the list—obfuscation, or fudging the issue—since it seems to be such an ingrained characteristic of Canadian declaratory policy on the American connection.[59] That this is so is a reflection once more of the diversity of the views and interests of the government's various domestic constituencies as well as of the requirements of international diplomacy. As prevalent and important as such strategems may be, however, they ultimately seek not to solve the problem, but to bury it, and hence do not qualify as genuine ''counter-integrative techniques.''

To repeat, no single one of the five basic strategies is adequate by itself as a foundation for dealing, on the Canadian side, with the continental question. In the real world of government policy, all of them must be deployed in varying combinations—as leaders desire, circumstances allow, and opportunities suggest. It is clear, nonetheless, that they are likely to remain as enduring features of the Canadian approach to the management of the American relationship. So also are the various "schools of protest" to which they are, in part, a response. For Canadians, in short, continentalism in North America is not merely an item on the current agenda of public policy, but a permanent condition of political life.

NOTES

[1] This is a slightly revised version of an oral presentation to the London seminar, for which the author had not been expected to prepare a formal paper. The medium—*pace* McLuhan—is not always the message, but it is still true that a good essay rarely comes from a fast speech. I hope readers will bear in mind that what follows was first intended as a stimulus to seminar discussion, and not as an academically systematic treatment of the subject. They should know as well that the first persons to suffer through the manuscript were Professors James Eayrs of Dalhousie and John Kirton of the University of Toronto, both of whom offered enormously helpful comments. Constraints of time prevented me from acting on them all as fully as I would have liked, but I am grateful to them both for assisting me to escape at least a few of my blunders.

[2] The continental reference throughout is to the area north of the Rio Grande. Some of Mexico's problems in dealing with the United States are similar to those of Canada, but the Mexican situation has not been included in the analysis.

[3] For a relatively recent statement, see Peyton V. Lyon, *Canada-United States Free Trade and Canadian Independence*, Economic Council Research Study (Ottawa: Information Canada, 1975). See also the Council's own report, *Looking Outward: A New Trade Strategy for Canada* (Ottawa: Information Canada, 1975).

[4] Most recently from the Standing Committee on Foreign Affairs of the Canadian Senate. See its report entitled *Canada-United States Relations: Volume II—Canada's Trade Relations with the United States* (Ottawa: Minister of Supply and Services Canada, 1978), especially pp. 112-24. I am indebted to James Eayrs for the observation that Canadian creative artists occasionally exhibit similar inclinations. Mordecai Richler, the novelist, is an indefatigable example.

[5] The two M.L.A.'s were, respectively, Richard Collver and Dennis Ham, and they have since established a "Unionest Party" (*sic*) to promote their cause. Their "continentalism" is partial, of course, since they do not presume to speak for Canada as a whole. Amalgamation in the West alone will do.

[6] It should be understood that the various schools are here being distinguished analytically, not organizationally or in terms of personnel. The same individuals are often prominent in more than one line of nationalist advocacy.

[7] Most popularly in two books by James M. Minifie, then the CBC's correspondent in Washington: *Peacemaker or Powder-Monkey: Canada's Role in a Revolutionary World* (Toronto: McClelland and Stewart, 1960), and *Open at the Top: Reflections on U.S.-Canada Relations* (Toronto: McClelland and Stewart, 1964).

[8] Stephen Clarkson, ed., *An Independent Foreign Policy for Canada?* (Toronto: McClelland and Stewart for the University League for Social Reform, 1968). The contributions originated

as a series of seminar papers presented in 1966-67. A number of External Affairs Department officials attended the proceedings, and the manuscripts subsequently became the starting point for an in-house review of Canadian foreign policy. The review was completed in the spring of 1968, just as the Pearson government was on the point of leaving office.

[9] A succinct statement of the argument can be found in Stephen Clarkson's ''The Choice to Be Made,'' *An Independent Foreign Policy for Canada?, op. cit.*, pp. 253-69.

[10] Charles Taylor (Toronto: Anansi, 1974).

[11] A clear statement of this position can be found in Peyton V. Lyon's rebuttal of Minifie's first volume. See his *The Policy Question: A Critical Appraisal of Canada's Role in World Affairs* (Toronto: McClelland and Stewart, 1963). An interesting official treatment appeared in the form of a joint report by A.D.P. Heeney, the Canadian Ambassador to the United States, and Livingston T. Merchant, the American Ambassador to Canada, under the title *Canada and the United States: Principles for Partnership* (Ottawa: Queen's Printer, 1965). The report aroused a measure of public controversy, and Mr. Heeney later defended it in a number of publications. See his ''Dealing with Uncle Sam,'' in *Canada's Role as a Middle Power*, edited by J. King Gordon (Toronto: Canadian Institute of International Affairs, 1966), pp. 87-100; and *The Things That Are Caesar's: Memoirs of a Canadian Public Servant* (Toronto: University of Toronto Press, 1972), especially pp. 190-200. He also received support from Peyton Lyon—a maverick contributor to the Clarkson connection—in his ''Quiet Diplomacy Revisited,'' in *An Independent Foreign Policy for Canada?, op. cit.*, pp. 29-41.

[12] See Kal J. Holsti, ''Canada and the United States,'' in *Conflict in World Politics*, edited by Steven Spiegel and Kenneth Waltz (Boston: Winthrop, 1971). pp. 375-96.

[13] Kal J. Holsti and Thomas Allen Levy, ''Bilateral Institutions and Transgovernmental Relation Between Canada and the United States,'' *International Organization* 28 (Autumn 1974): 875-901, especially pp. 896-97. How permanent the change actually was is difficult to say.

[14] These, too, of course, can be regarded as a confining form of penetration—an argument that underlay much of the discussion in the Minifie books, and can be found in other sources as well, including, for example, John W. Warnock's *Parner to Behemoth: The Military Policy of a Satellite Canada* (Toronto: New Press, 1970), and the studies by Lewis Hertzman, John Warnock, and Thomas Hockin in their *Alliances & Illusions: Canada and the NATO-NORAD Question* (Edmonton: Hurtig, 1969).

[15] Canada, House of Commons, Standing Committee on External Affairs and National Defence, *Minutes of Proceedings and Evidence* (20 November, 1969), p. 64.

[16] *Ibid.*, p. 66

[17] Roger Frank Swanson, *State/Provincial Interaction: A Study of Relations Between U.S. States and Canadian Provinces Prepared for the U.S. Department of State* (Washington, D.C.: The Canus Research Institute, August 1974). See also Kal J. Holsti and Thomas Allen Levy, *op. cit.*, and Thomas Levy and Don Munton, ''Federal-Provincial Dimensions of State-Provincial Relations,'' *International Perspectives* 5 (March/April 1976): 23-27. An excellent review of the literature on the phenomenon is contained in Maureen Appel Molot, ''Intergovernmental Relations Between Canadian Provinces and U.S. States: The Canadian View,'' paper prepared for the Institute of Public Administration of Canada Annual Conference, Halifax, September 1976.

[18] See, for example, Hertzman, Warnock, and Hockin, *op. cit*.

[19] For most of these summary figures I am indebted to Abraham Rotstein's "Canada: The New Nationalism," *Foreign Affairs* 55 (October 1976): 97-118.

[20] For background, see Denis Smith, *Gentle Patriot: A Politcal Biography of Walter Gordon* (Edmonton: Hurtig, 1973), especially Chapter 2.

[21] *Foreign Ownership and the Structure of Canadian Industry: Report of the Task Force on the Structure of Canadian Industry* (Ottawa: Privy Council Office, January 1968). The head of the task force was Melville H. Watkins, a University of Toronto economist who was radicalized by the experience. See Dave Godfrey and Mel Watkins, eds., *Gordon to Watkins to You, Documentary: The Battle for Control of Our Economy* (Toronto: New Press, 1970).

[22] Which they might not be prepared to do if the competition were with the parent firm or with other subsidiaries of the same corporation.

[23] Instead of simply importing the practical results of laboratory research conducted by the parent in the United States or elsewhere.

[24] As opposed to the level of mere subsidiary management.

[25] There was evidence to suggest that in some fields the presence in the relatively small Canadian market of subsidiary producers for each of the principal multinational firms abroad meant that no single one of them could operate with suffecient volume to ensure peak efficiency.

[26] An obligation that could be evaded through internal pricing arrangements, especially in cases where components were imported from foreign branches of the same enterprises, and where there was profit advantage in shifting book profits, and hence tax liability, to a foreign tax jurisdiction. It should be understood, in fairness to the Gordon school, that the foregoing list of rather materialistic preoccupations has the effect of unjustly cheapening the arguments of its supporters, who have been very much concerned with wider questions bearing on the quality and integrity of Canadian life. The fact remains, however, that they have considered the pattern of foreign investment to be the principal causal mechanism, and hence the primary focus of remedial action.

[27] In the past, this problem has arisen for Canada primarily in relation to trade with Communist powers like Cuba and China. The true significance of the difficulty is hard to measure, however, since it seems probable that many subsidiaries of American firms avoid even raising the issue because they anticipate the opposition of the United States government and/or the parent corporation. The effect of the legislation on Canadian exports is therefore largely invisible.

[28] Through the activities of the so-called "Waffle Group," in which Professor Watkins was a leading figure. The group was successful in sensitizing the party to the issue, but its attempt to secure a full endorsement of its position ultimately failed.

[29] One of the most widely cited studies is Kari Levitt's *Silent Surrender: The Multinational Corporation in Canada* (Toronto: Macmillan, 1970). Some of the collections of essays arising from the seminars of the University League for Social Reform at the University of Toronto—the same group that was responsible for *An Independent Foreign Policy for Canada?*—contain articles on the subject. See especially Peter Russell, ed., *Nationalism in Canada* (Toronto:

McGraw-Hill, 1966), and Ian Lumsden, ed., *Close the 49th Parallel Etc.: The Americanization of Canada* (Toronto: University of Toronto Press, 1970). A prominent intellectual, as well as organizational, leader of the nationalist movement has been Abraham Rotstein, also of the University of Toronto, who has published a collection of his essays under the title *The Precarious Homestead: Essays on Economics, Technology and Nationalism* (Toronto: New Press, 1973). Professor Rotstein was for some years the editor of *The Canadian Forum*, the leading periodical of Canadian intellectual nationalists and was succeeded in that position by Denis Smith, the biographer of Walter Gordon. A number of publications have also appeared under the auspices of the Committee for an Independent Canada, a pressure group operating in support of nationalist causes, and including representatives from the major Canadian political parties. See, for example, Abraham Rotstein and Gary Lax, eds., *Independence: The Canadian Challenge* (Toronto: McClelland and Stewart for the Committee for an Independent Canada, 1972). Uninitiated readers who are struck by the frequency with which the same names appear in these various contexts would be quite right in concluding that the sociology of the Canadian nationalist movement is a subject worthy of investigation in itself. So also are its connections with political parties, pressure groups, indigenous book and magazine publishers, and the communications media at large.

[30] See, in particular, Wallace Clement, *Continental Corporate Power: Economic Linkages Between Canada and the United States* (Toronto: McClelland and Stewart, 1977).

[31] Abraham Rotstein, Interview, 24 May 1973.

[32] Perhaps the best known, and certainly the most acerbic, proponent of this position was the late Harry G. Johnson. For examples, see the essays in his *The Canadian Quandary: Economic Problems and Policies* (Toronto: McGraw-Hill, 1963).

[33] Rotstein, "Canada: The New Nationalism," *op. cit.,* pp. 97−98. The issue of the Americanization of the Canadian academic community is canvassed on the nationalist side by Robin Mathews and James Steele, eds., in *The Struggle for Canadian Universities* (Toronto: New Press, 1969). This concern has been accompanied by a preoccupation with the fate of "Canadian studies." See T.H.B. Symons, *To Know Ourselves: The Report of the Commission on Canadian Studies*, Vols. I and II (Ottawa: AUCC, 1975). Not surprisingly, much of the attention has focused on the social sciences. Consider, for example, George Grant's "The University Curriculum," in his *Technology and Empire: Perspectives on North America* (Toronto: Anansi, 1969), pp. 111-34; Ellen Wood and Neal Wood, "Canada and the American Science of Politics," in Lumsden, *op. cit.*, pp. 179-95; and Melville H. Watkins, "The Dismal State of Economics in Canada," *ibid.*, pp. 197-208.

[34] It should be understood, again, that not all those who have become involved in this issue necessarily have motives so purely rooted in theoretical premises. In the cultural field, as in the economic, it is possible to argue that nationalism has become in Canada a very profitable business, and more than a few of its adherents have personal stakes in the outcome.

[35] For samples and further references, see Janice L. Murray, *Canadian Cultural Nationalism: The Fourth Lester B. Pearson Conference on the Canada-U.S. Relationship* (New York: New York University Press for the Canadian Institute of International Affairs and the Council on Foreign Relations, 1977).

[36] See, for example several treatments by T. Joseph Scanlon, including "The Sources of Foreign News in Canadian Daily Newspapers" (a report prepared for the press and liaison division, Department of External Affairs, 20 December 1967); "A Study of the Contents of 30

Canadian Daily Newspapers'' (prepared for the Special Senate Committee on Mass Media, Ottawa, 1969); and ''Canada Sees the World Through U.S. Eyes: One Case Study in Cultural Domination,'' *The Canadian Forum* (September 1974): 34-39. See also Rick A. Butler, ''News Agencies in Canada: An Analysis of Informational Dependency'' (paper presented at the 47th annual meeting of the Canadian Political Science Association, Edmonton, 2-5 June 1975); Jim A. Hart, ''The Flows of News Between the United States and Canada,'' *Journalism Quarterly* 40 (Winter 1963): 70-74; Benjamin D. Singer, ''American Invasion of the Mass Media in Canada,'' in *Critical Issues in Canadian Society*, edited by Craig L. Boydell, Carl F. Grindstaff, and Paul C. Whitehead (Toronto: Holt, Rinehart and Winston, 1971), pp. 423-26; and Vernone M. Sparkes, ''The Flow of News Between Canada and the United States,'' *Journalism Quarterly* 55 (Summer 1978):260-68. For similar discussions of French-language newspapers in Quebec, see André P. Donneur, ''La presse du Québec et les pays étrangers,'' *Études Internationales* 2 (September 1971): 410-23, and Jean-Pierre Rogel, ''La presse québécoise et l'information sur la politique internationale,'' Études Internationales 5 (December 1974): 693-711. On the government side, see Special Senate Committee on Mass Media, *Report on Mass Media: Vol. I—The Uncertain Mirror* (Ottawa: Information Canada, 1970), especially pp. 233-35.

[37] The principal factors underlying the lack of Canadian foreign correspondents are the cost, together with the relative lack of reader interest. The problem is complicated by the fact that the multiplicity of Canadian time zones makes it difficult for any single newspaper to serve the entire country. The small ''attentive public'' is scattered in the various cities, making the development of a ''quality press,'' suitable for the sophisticated market, an uneconomic prospect. No increase in advertising revenue can be expected to accrue to a publisher simply because he asks his editors to increase their coverage of foreign news.

[38] Some of the latter would argue, of course, that patterns of news dependency are simply additional manifestations of economic penetration. It has been suggested to me as well that informational penetration may not be conceptually distinguishable from cultural penetration, and that in any case the category has been defined much too narrowly. It might be extended, for example, to include the accelerating transborder operations of computerized data-banking and data-processing, which have recently become a matter of great concern, and which similarly reflect the web-like development of transnational enterprises and technologies. I concede that the category needs more thought. Certainly its boundaries require better definition.

[39] Such inhibitions have not afflicted the press in Western Europe, however. See Anthony Smith, *Subsidies and the Press in Europe* (London: PEP in association with the International Press Institute, June 1977).

[40] Interestingly, the difficulties between English- and French-Canada have intensified as these conceptions have weakened. This is partly because the decline of traditional values among Québécois has altered their vocational preferences and has brought them for the first time into areas in which they are in direct conflict with their already entrenched English-speaking counterparts.

[41] Subtitled, *The Defeat of Canadian Nationalism* (Toronto: McClelland and Stewart, 1965). More sophisticated statements of Grant's position on these questions can be found in his collection of essays, *Technology and Empire: Perspectives on North America* (Toronto: Anansi, 1969).

[42] It is easy to draw any of a multitude of cause-and-effect linkages here. For example, economic penetration may generate commercial advertising campaigns, which in turn can

profoundly influence life-styles and values. Marxists, of course, find no difficulty in establishing the interlocking character of the forces involved.

[43] The exception may be the province of Quebec, but supporters of national unity may not think this especially helpful. Quebec cars, for example, carry the phrase "Je me souviens" on their licence plates, but part of what their drivers remember is the British conquest.

[44] Such studies are founded, of course, on the European unity movement, but on the Canadian side of the border they tend to have the opposite normative flavour. The integrative processes involved are seen, that is, as menacing rather than constructive.

[45] Naomi Black, "Absorptive Systems Are Impossible: The Canadian-American Relationship as a Disparate Dyad," in *Continental Community? Independence & Integration in North America*, edited by Andrew Axline, James E. Hyndman, Peyton V. Lyon, and Maureen A. Molot (Toronto: McClelland and Stewart, 1974). The essays in this book are all designed to consider the integration thesis in the Canada-U.S. context.

[46] See Peyton V. Lyon and Brian W. Tomlin, *Canada as an International Actor* (Toronto: Macmillan, 1979), especially Chapter 6, "Canada-U.S. Integration," pp. 95-121. They distinguish seven "dimensions" of integration, and their taxonomy cuts across the categories employed in the present analysis. The dimensions are (1) formal economic; (2) institutional; (3) transactional; (4) policy; (5) transnational; (6) attitudinal; and (7) cultural. Charles Pentland, in *Continental Community? Independence and Integration in North America*, edited by W.A. Axline *et al.* (Toronto: McClelland and Stewart, 1974), suggests five: (1) coercive power; (2) decision making; (3) functional administration; (4) socio-political communication; and (5) attitude. See especially pp. 42-57. I am indebted to Professor David Leyton-Brown for drawing attention to this characteristic of the integration theory literature in his "Perspectives on Canadian-American Relations: The Scope of the Literature," paper presented to the Inter-University Seminar on International Relations, University of Ottawa, 7-8 March, 1980.

[47] See Robert O. Keohane and Joseph S. Nye, Jr., eds., "Transnational Relations and World Politics," *International Organization* 25 (Summer 1971); subsquently published as a book by Harvard University Press in 1972.

[48] Transgovernmental activities refer to "direct interactions between agencies (governmental subunits) of different governments where those agencies act relatively autonomously from central government control." See Robert O. Keohane and Joseph S. Nye, Jr., "Introduction: The Complex Politics of Canadian-American Interdependence," *International Organization* 28 (Autumn 1974), p. 596. For a full-dress treatment of the organizational structures involved, see Roger Frank Swanson, *Intergovernmental Perspectives on the Canada-U.S. Relationship* (New York: New York University Press, 1978).

[49] Keohane and Nye, "Introduction," *op. cit.*

[50] See Annette Baker Fox and Alfred O. Hero, Jr., "Canada and the United States: Their Binding Frontier," *International Organization* 28 (Autumn 1974): 999-1014.

[51] Systems analysts in this context are concerned with the thesis that the behaviour of states is determined by the membership and structural characteristics of the international system and by the places respectively of different countries within it. This implies a "billiard-ball" model of international politics, however, and hence in its simplest form does not deal effectively with problems arising from the phenomenon of "penetration." If penetrative phenomena are to be

accommodated, the systems concept has to be greatly elaborated with 'sub-system' additions. See, for example, John H. Redekop, ''A Reinterpretation of Canadian-American Relations,'' *Canadian Journal of Political Science* 9 (June 1976):227-43. For commentaries, see David Leyton-Brown, *op. cit.*, and Elizabeth Smythe, ''International Relations Theory and the Study of Canadian-American Relations,'' *Canadian Journal of Political Science* 13 (March 1980):121-47.

[52] See, for example, James Eayrs, ''Canada and the United States: The Politics of Disparate Power,'' *The Centennial Review* 10 (Fall 1966):415-29, for the argument that ''the most significant political fact about the relations of (Canada and the United States) is that one of them is so very much more powerful than the other—reckoning the constituents of power by almost any index.''

[53] Most of the following discussion is abstracted from a paper entitled, ''Towards a Canadian Foreign Policy for the 1980s: Defining Canadian Interests,'' presented to a Progressive Conservative conference on foreign policy (Toronto, January 1979). The brevity of the Conservatives' subsequent period in office suggests that they may not have found it very helpful.

[54] Canadian governments do not formally espouse anything that could be recognized as an ''America policy.'' Comprehensive characterizations are therefore possible only in restrospect. The first Trudeau government did, however, publish a general statement on the subject. See Mitchell Sharp, ''Canada-U.S. Relations: Options for the Future,'' *International Perspectives* 1 (Special Issue—Autumn 1972):1-24.

[55] It should be understood that these strategies include most of, but are not exhausted by, the remedial policies suggested by the various ''schools of protest.'' Some are inventions of a beleaguered officialdom. I should perhaps add that I have given some thought to appending an additional strategic category under the label, ''bilateral institutionalization,'' to refer essentially to organizations established jointly by the two countries to administer, regulate, or advise upon certain aspects of the bilateral relationship. To the extent that these are effective, they may act partly as ''equalizers'' by removing issues from the sphere of normal diplomatic bargaining and subjecting them to resolution by reference primarily to technical and administrative criteria. See, again, Kal J. Holsti and Thomas Allen Levy, ''Bilateral Institutions and Transgovernmental Relations Between Canada and the United States,'' *op. cit.*, especially pp. 877-81 and 896-901. For detailed treatments of some of the more prominent examples, consult William R. Willoughby, *The Joint Organizations of Canada and the United States* (Toronto: University of Toronto Press, 1979). The difficulty is that such arrangements can be viewed more readily as ''integrative'' than as ''counter-integrative'' instruments.

[56] On the other hand, it can be argued with considerable persuasiveness that to attempt to co-ordinate the entire conduct of Canada's relations with the United States would be administratively as well as politically and diplomatically impracticable. Even if the necessary domestic consensus could be obtained, and even if the Americans were prepared to take no inconvenient notice, such a process might well break down as a result of ''co-ordination overload.'' Some forms of confusion are functionally useful.

[57] Difficulties of this sort could easily arise, for example, over the export to the United States of energy, raw materials, and perhaps most significantly for the future, water.

[58] This issue has a long and complex history, and it has produced a voluminous literature in itself. See, for example, Isaiah Litvak and Christopher Maule, *Cultural Sovereignty: The Time and Reader's Digest Case in Canada* (New York: Praeger, 1974).

[59] An amusing example is provided by the central policy recommendation in Mitchell Sharp's "Canada-U.S. Relations: Options for the Future," *op. cit.* After a generally impressive analysis of the problem itself, the paper concludes that Canada should "pursue a comprehensive, long-term strategy to develop and strengthen the Canadian economy and other aspects of our national life and in the process to reduce the present Canadian vulnerability." This is known elsewhere as having one's cake and eating it, too.

Chapter Six

National Politics and Supranational Integration

by
Helen Wallace

Academic theory and political practice appear to have turned a complete circle in the context of European integration. In the 1950s and early 1960s, most analysts of the European Community (EC) argued persuasively that the momentum of integration was displacing the nation-state as the fulcrum of political activity. The empirical record of the EC was impressive and seemed to substantiate the arguments of the theorists. By the mid-1960s, the seeds of doubt had been sown. Acute controversy within the EC began to suggest that governments wanted and could have their cake and eat it. Member states generated support for intensive co-operation on many issues, yet national sovereignty had enough resilience to preserve strong national identities. Governments stood back from relinquishing authority to the EC on other issues and were reluctant to extend the scope of collaboration. The French were alone in asserting this explicitly as a point of principle. But the other governments showed case by case their hesitancy to co-operate except where their national interests clearly converged with what the EC collectively embraced. This seemed to vindicate those more sceptical academics who had consistently argued that the EC could never be more than an intergovernmental creation, the servant and not the master of its members.[1]

During the 1970s, this view gained currency as the only viable explanation of the EC. Integration disappeared as the organizing concept of the theorists, to be replaced by the more diffuse labels of transnationalism and interdependence. The disarray of that decade, exemplified in the shock of a deepening recession, even suggested that the member states were beginning to retract what they had already conceded. Preference for individual national policies was strong. The EC was apparently left as simply one of many international forums for consultation and sporadic co-ordination. The old policies of the 1950s and 1960s survived, but were barely adjusted to take account of their changing economic environment. No one could deny that economic interdependence had severely constrained national policies, but this phenomenon spread wider than the EC. What was less clear was whether the Community experiment had done more than intensify the need for its members to consult more regularly than was required in other forums.

Yet there were paradoxes. The scope of co-operation was extended to include foreign policy consultations in 1970 and the creation of the European Monetary System (EMS) in 1979. The scope of the institutions grew with the meetings of heads of government in the European Council and more surprisingly with a strengthened European Parliament that by 1979 was elected by direct suffrage. The membership of the EC was expanded in 1973 and is about to be further increased. Outside observers have stood back in confusion, reluctant to categorize the essence of the Community's character, and uncertain as to whether the 1980s would see a revival of creativity and a resurgence of integrative pressures or a dilution into a looser association variously labelled as "two tier" or "à la carte!"[2]

In the midst of this confusion, a crucial point has become clear. Balanced analysis of the Community depends on a careful assessment of its impact on its component parts. Unless we can understand the response of the member states to their participation, we shall fail to determine whether there is a distinct phenomenon affecting relations among nations within the Community and influencing the course of national politics and policies. Regrettably, however, the territory is still not fully charted. A number of studies have been made of particular aspects of the interrelationships between the member states and the EC.[3] There are some assessments of individual national policies.[4] But the coverage is far from complete and there is no accepted framework for evaluating their findings. Perhaps most striking is the extent to which studies of domestic politics within the individual countries that happen to be members of the EC still neglect the Community (and indeed international obligations in general) as a relevant dimension. Their justification may correctly be that what happens internally is still of primary importance. However, the reality of interdependence in both the economic and security domains nonetheless impinges on domestic policy options and has, in consequence, a political significance.

In order to come closer to evaluating the character of the Community, we need to address three main questions:

1. Is the impact of the EC on its members different in kind from that of other forms of international co-operation?
2. What is the nature of the Community's impact on the politics of its members?
3. What are the factors that determine the way in which member states respond to the EC?

THE IDIOSYNCRACY OF THE COMMUNITY

The first question is the simplest. Both academic research and the political record agree in defining the Community as different in kind from the other international associations to which its members belong.[5] The Community method, derived from the treaty framework and the operations of independent institutions, ties the member states into an intensity and range of organized co-operation that are unparalleled in other international organizations. Here the theorists, especially the neo-functionalists, were quite right to draw attention to the subtleties of the bargaining process, to the importance of interactions among national élites, to the characteristics of policy co-operation in prescribed sectors, and to the resources that can be mobilized in support of Community goals. A cross-national policy consensus is still difficult to achieve, and agreements are not progressively cumulative or unilinear. Yet the Community system, in spite of all of its problems, has proved remarkably resilient. It has been capable of generating accord, often to the surprise of its participants.

The consequence is that the EC bites deeply into national policy processes. It sets constraints on national freedom of manoeuvre. It offers opportunities for individual members to mobilize Community resources in support of national policy objectives, most evident in the agricultural sector. It allows member governments to deflect criticism by arguing that the burden of responsibility lies at the Community rather than the national level. The rules of the Community game have become quite firmly established in a set of norms about legitimate behaviour. Certainly the rules can be manipulated to national advantage depending on the dexterity of the players. But it is rare for the rules to be openly flouted.[6] Moreover, it is evident that the nature of bargaining in the EC is essentially political—the politics of money, of resource allocation, of rule enforcement, of interest articulation and aggregation, all issue areas recognized by the standard works on political science as key attributes of a political sytem.

Yet the institutional framework remains only partly formed. Community institutions have a momentum of their own. The Commission's powers and status may be less than its protagonists would like, but its role in decision making remains of primary importance. The Court of Justice has established both authority and capacity for extending the scope of common legislation. The Parliament now holds the elements of democratic accountability and at a minimum has acquired the power to be awkward. But the contortions involved in reaching a consensus in the Council of Ministers illustrate the limitations of the system. There is not the degree of authority or legitimacy within the Community institutions that yet fosters an independent form of government. Instead, agreement consolidated through a common framework permits shared management of partially common programmes. Thus Community decision making has extended the governments of its members into a new dimension, but without displacing government at the national level. Community government coexists with national government but cannot be separated from it. It remains dependent on what politics within individual member states will permit. Yet the autonomy of national governments is circumscribed by their obligations to each other and by a shared commitment to preserve the common ground that has been established.

Perhaps most striking is the extent to which particular domestic interests have become vested in the Community enterprise. The overall achievements of common agreement are encapsulated in the so-called *acquis communautaire*, a phrase that summarizes the core of treaty commitments and common legislations so far adopted. This collective property is, however, an amalgam of those individual vested interests—*droits acquis*—that governments have successfully woven into the fabric of a Community consensus. The *acquis communautaire* not only survives but is reinforced by the concern of its beneficiaries to ensure that the rewards of Community co-operation continue to flow. Herein lies the essence of national interest in the context of Community bargaining. Community politics, like national politics, consists of a framework and a process through which the participants seek to attain their separate objectives and to conserve the status and material gains that they regard as appropriate. The Community is authoritative and legitimate to the extent that it can balance the needs and interests of its members within an acceptable package of rewards and burdens. The Community made rapid progress in the 1950s and 1960s because its founders and their heirs were able to strike and maintain a compact that contained sufficiently attractive rewards to cajole its members into accepting some penalties.

During the late 1960s and the 1970s, the compact came under threat. The initial core of agreement was limited in that it was confined to a few priority issues. These were originally accepted by members because they converged with what were then their individual national priorities. But the economic environment changed, the priorities of individual governments began to diversify, and enlargement brought into the Community member states with different views about the core of the common enterprise. It became increasingly evident that member states differed on crucial questions of economic doctrine so much that national policies could not easily coalesce around common positions that would take the Community into new areas. As these shifts occurred and coincided, the seeds of instability were sown. The Community became susceptible to charges of obsolescence, imbalance, and inappropriateness in terms of the sum of interests that were relevant to its members. There are elements of obsolescence in the ideological presuppositions of Community philosophy faced with economic recession rather than steady growth. There is imbalance in the continuing emphasis on agriculture and tariffs in a period of industrial retraction and acute energy dependence. There is inappropriateness in the perverseness of the impact of current policies on some member states and in the lack of consensus on measures to foster economic convergence among member states with widely different economic performance (about to be emphasized by a further round of enlargement). There is, at the least, a question mark over the stress of Community policies on often rather narrow and sectional interests in a period of international political tension.

The consequence is that a wedge has been driven among the member states and between different sections of opinion within the member states. The strongest support for the old Community idea comes from those whose interests are vested in its practical manifestations—notably the farmers and traders, who continue to benefit, and their advocates inside individual governments. The criticisms and counter-proposals spring from those who see their interests as either neglected or threatened by current EC policies, whether consumers of food, French sheep farmers, industries at risk, or the British more generally as they deplore the impact of the EC budget on the United Kingdom. This is not to suggest that the Community has relapsed into a narrow forum for the pursuit of material interest. All political systems depend for their stability on their ability to satisfy the material needs of their citizens.

But it is no accident that the Commission and the European Parliament have separately reached the conclusion that some of the old policies must change and new policies must be developed. Both institutions have the advantage of irresponsibility that makes it easier for them to escape the defence of the *status quo* than is possible for individual governments that seek re-election. Here the Community is at a great disadvantage precisely because its policy coverage remains limited. It does not yet have the resources or capacity to meet the aggregate interests of all the member states across the full range of major policy sectors. Governments can live with this because they retain the ability to develop separate national policies irrespective of and sometimes in spite of the Community. Indeed, in many cases that range from the narrow technical issues of standards for lawn-mowers to big questions of foreign policy, they prefer to rely on national actions because they do not believe that policy at the EC level is likely to reflect their individual national objectives.

The Community is then a special form of international co-operation precisely because its common legislation has direct policy effects on the member states and because it offers the opportunity for the pursuit of specific interests through collective action. In many ways it seems to resemble a domestic political system. Yet it has not made the breakthrough to an incontrovertibly integrated form, nor has it been able to construct common policies in the main area of political and economic concern outside agriculture and the customs union. Its vigour depends on how far its common policies command acceptance from and remain relevant to its clients. A strong element of conditionality is still attached to the maintenance of momentum within the Community. So long as the rewards of participation, both tangible and intangible, continue to flow, then its foundations remain firm. But they will not necessarily induce support for extensions to either the scope or the authority of the Community *vis-à-vis* its member governments. Integration does not proceed by stealth but by its ability to deliver a mixture of benefits enticing enough to justify the constraints on national autonomy that inevitably accompany common policies.

THE IMPACT OF THE COMMUNITY ON NATIONAL POLITICS

The theoretical literature of the 1950s and 1960s did not produce a consensus on the political prerequisites of supranational integration. Functionalists and neo-functionalists emphasized the importance for the Community of attracting the political support of policy-making élites and economic interest groups in the member states. The transactionalists and intergovernmentalists argued from their different standpoints that the Community would not have political legitimacy unless ·and until it commanded the political loyalty of a wider public. The lessons of experience suggest that the two requirements are complementary rather than contradictory.

During the 1950s and early 1960s, the supranational experiment in Western Europe drew into active collaboration significant sections of national policy élites. In some sectors, notably agriculture, it engaged the positive support of the *clientele* of Community policies. The circle of those involved remained limited, and within this confined network of national interest groups, officials, and politicians, rapid progress occurred in the construction of common policies that served their collective interests. This joint and élite enterprise rested on a foundation of popular support. A permissive consensus throughout the six founder countries enabled substantial transfers of power to take place from the national to the Community level. This achievement seemed solid enough to generate confidence in the prospect of gradually extending the model to encompass other sectors too. But this did not happen on a scale commensurate with the promise of the common agricultural policy or the customs union. Building blocks have been set in place, but both the design and the construction of other policies remain incomplete. Part of the explanation for this discontinuity lies in the character of both the élite interactions and the permissive consensus.

The neo-functionalists suggested that national élites would bargain with each other in the Community in such a way that Community policies would aggregate their various interests. They borrowed from the functionalists the view that within particular policy sectors, a technocratic rationale would bind together policy makers irrespective of their different national origins. But they refined the argument with the claim that it would be possible to construct packages of advantages that would benefit groups with diverse interests, provided that the Community was active simultaneously in several areas of policy. They recognized that priorities would differ, but believed that they would be compatible within an amalgam of linked agreements. During the 1950s and 1960s, the hypothesis held good. It was helped by a favourable economic environment that produced a steadily expanding cake, which broadly allowed a maximization of benefits at both national and Community levels. It was not challenged by ideological rifts about the role of the state or over economic doctrine. This is not to say that all sections within the member states benefited materially from Community policies or to deny that there were alternative critiques of the centrist and largely *laissez-faire* orthodoxy. But these factors did not impinge on the core of the Community compact, nor did they figure prominently in the evaluations by member of the assets of EC co-operation.

Towards the end of the 1960s, this began to change. Once the Community began to grope towards regional and industrial policies, it became clear that national economic doctrines were not entirely compatible in respect of either objectives or instruments.[7] The sectional interests concerned were anxious about their competitive position and lacked the confidence in the Community as their protector or disinterested arbiter that had facilitated co-operation in agriculture. There was dissension among policy makers on options and priorities, strikingly different from the congruence of attitudes on the key elements of agricultural policy. The Community was hampered in its efforts to jump from sectoral policies to "global" policies. Economic and monetary union proved unattainable in the short to medium term because of the subjective differences in national philosophies and the objective divergences in economic performance.[8] While the intensity of interaction among national policy élites grew, it was not accompanied by a convergence of attitudes and policy. The habit of consultation became ingrained, but it kept the participants acutely aware of the differences—both subjective and objective—that separated them. This was reflected in the growing emphasis on the co-ordination of national policies as distinct from their replacement by single and common policies.

As the recession of the 1970s accentuated, so national policy makers recognized their common predicament, but fell back on the familiar prop of separate national policies, even while they admitted the limitations of this approach. By the latter part of the decade, the trend was marginally reversed as the EC established the European Monetary System and some common programmes for industries in crisis. But their scope was limited, their objectives were modest, and their advocates were cautious, a marked contrast with the optimism, ambition, and creativity of the early years of the EC. These policies had elements of burden sharing but without the maximization of mutual advantage that had characterized the first phase in the Community's history. By and large the Community retained its *acquis* with the majority of its membership committed to consolidating what had already been agreed. But even among the more enthusiastic governments, the time-scale for progress in other areas was lengthened.

This phenomenon reflects not just the changing attitudes of policy makers within the member governments. It derives in large measure from a change in the basis of popular support for the Community experiment. The creation of the EC was fostered by a broad public acceptance of the inadequacy of the nation-state and of the need for economic and political reconstruction via the medium of international, even supranational, co-operation. This was supplemented by the belief of significant sectional interests that Community policies offered positive benefits by comparison with national policies. Some groups even switched from antagonism to tolerance of Community interference as they identified their material improvement with the fruits of Community endeavour.[9] Large segments of the populations of the member states were barely affected in a direct sense by Community activities. But as long as economic expansion continued, they were susceptible to persuasion that the mere existence of the Community had facilitated their welfare gains, even if the causal relationship could not be incontestably established. The permissive consensus thus comprised a mixture of active support by some with passive acceptance by most of the Community *per se*. It meant that transfers of political authority to EC institutions could be interpreted as an extension of national sovereignty rather than a threat to it.

But this too changed. Much of the early rationale for the creation of the EC had diminished in force by the 1970s, perhaps largely because it could be taken for granted. The danger of civil war in Western Europe seemed to have been averted. The establishment of international regimes for economic co-operation had been accomplished, even if they were subject to strains. The restraints on economic development made particular groups more defensive and anxious to conserve their positions *vis-à-vis* others both within their own countries and in other countries.[10] In some countries that were undergoing economic strains, politics also became more polarized, with sharp debate over alternative economic policies that sat uneasily with the middle-of-the-road consensus that had characterized Community orthodoxy.[11] The Community context became a framework of competition and conflict rather than a forum for the pursuit of readily compatible common interests.

The consequence is that Community bargaining is now more politicized. At the Community level, negotiations over priorities, resource allocation, and the instruments of policy have become more intense. It is more difficult to reach agreement on particular policy programmes without a consensus on objectives and principles. Yet the Community system lacks the political cohesion that would facilitate a consensus on fundamental values and choices. This is not to imply that the process of integration has been reversed, but rather to suggest that it is now encountering more crucial and awkward political dilemmas. Nor is it possible for governments in Community negotiations to yield ground to their partners, unless they are confident that they can carry the support of their domestic opinion.[12] The politics of the budget illustrate this phenomenon most explicitly, since revenue raising and the distribution of funds reflect most tangibly the differential advantages of Community policies for particular countries and for particular groups. Yet the allocation of money does not rest on a clear basis derived from underlying political principles, but rather on the disjointed pattern of benefits that has emerged somewhat erratically from a process of policy making that has been markedly more effective in the agricultural sector than in other economic sectors. The key issue that surrounds the current budget controversy is whether the Community will prove capable of transforming its finances into a pattern based on commonly shared principles politically acceptable to all of its members.[13] In parallel, there is conflict over the extent to which the Community level should have primacy over the national level in determining the content and modalities of "common" policies. This is reflected in difficulties over the degree of authority for Community institutions in managing policies, and over the question of whether Community money should support only common policies or rather endorse distinct national policies.[14]

The corollary is that within the member states, Community issues have become more strongly politicized. The vested interests of particular groups, notably the farmers who benefit from current EC policies, have had an impact on the distribution of political weight within national governments. In all of the member states, the political position of the agricultural lobby has been reinforced by the ability of their sponsors to exploit Community resources and to deploy leverage based on intra-Community bargaining. The lack of comparable advantage for many other sectional groups has begun to be reflected in pointed criticism of Community priorities, whether from the consumer of food and the taxpayer who carry the burden of agricultural finance, or from the industrial groups that identify their material interests with national rather than Community policies. In most member states, this has added an edge to domestic political debate, which makes the Community an awkward extra dimension.[15] It complicates national politics but without destabilizing them, as long as the vested interests of the beneficiaries of EC policies can be more or less conserved, and provided that national policies can still respond adequately to the needs of other groups. In the case of the United Kingdom, however, the position is more complex and even more highly politicized. Britain suffers from the double disadvantage that the current balance of Community policies is not congruent with the material interests of much of its population, while the scope for compensating domestic policies is limited by the slender economic resources available for national programmes.[16] Inevitably, therefore, the political and economic value of participation in the Community is more contested in Britain than in the other member states.

Two major political implications flow from this. First, each member government is engaged in Community negotiations with the object of ensuring that its national balance sheet contains more credit than debit. The items in the calculation include both tangible material benefits and non-quantifiable economic and political advantage, but a mixture of both is required to sustain a domestic political consensus favourable to the continuation and extension of Community co-operation. As economic circumstances have become less favourable, the need to secure substantive benefits has become more compelling. The intangible advantages may remain important, but they cannot provide a substitute. Secondly, the Community is unlikely to make any great leap forward in policy co-operation, unless it can establish a consensus on the issues that are at the top of the political and economic agendas of the member states. The problem is that the priority issues have become both more complex and less tractable than was the case in the 1950s and 1960s. The conservation of industries at risk, the development of new economic activities, the compensation for regional disadvantage, and the preservation of basic economic resources are all of central importance. But each requires difficult and controversial choices at the national level. To resolve them at the Community level depends on an acceptance by all the member states that the Community framework offers more than separate national policies can provide. As yet, both governments and their domestic publics lack the confidence that the Community is politically capable of meeting a challenge on this scale.

THE DETERMINANTS OF NATIONAL POLICIES

National policies on EC issues are determined by a blend of political and economic factors. They are formulated by member governments through national policy processes that modulate and interpret the relative weight of these various factors. The balance and priorities differ from one member state to another. In some, political and economic factors are aggregated into a coherent set of national objectives and policies. In others, internal contradictions confuse the definition of national interest. Two crucial questions follow. How far are the political and economic determinants of national policies congruent with the middle ground of the Community consensus? And how effective are individual governments in promoting their own definitions of the aims and instruments of proposed EC policies? Congruence is supportive of extensions of EC scope and authority, while incompatibilities generate reservations. Effectiveness or ''success'' by governments in rallying a Community-wide consensus behind their national aspirations depends on variables, difficult to pin down, that derive from national policy processes and the skills of national negotiators in exploiting the Community process. It may enable a government to put the onus on the rest of the Community to adjust rather than itself be compelled to alter its own preferences.

All analysts of the Community have found it difficult to evaluate the relative weights of economic and political factors. The functionalists and neo-functionalists emphasized welfare issues as the most appropriate subject matter for EC co-operation, on the assumption that economic integration once established would then permit a slide into political integration. The intergovernmentalists, by contrast, argued that welfare issues would remain subordinate to issues of high politics. History suggests that both approaches are distorted. Major political battles have repeatedly been fought over economic issues, and indeed the record suggests that fewer and fewer welfare issues can be insulated from political controversy. The stuff of Community politics is debate over economic policies and their implications. National perceptions of the politics of Community bargaining are rooted in assessments of economic advantage and disadvantage. Elements of ''pure'' politics barely creep into Community bargaining. Indeed, the whole EC system has camouflaged and suppressed overt political debate over policy choices and priorities. It is virtually unknown for Community decisions to be taken by explicit reference to partisan or ideological political choices of the kind that characterize domestic politics within the member states.

The essentially political features of the Community are still obscured by the technocratic shield behind which both member governments and Community institutions continue to find shelter. Partisanship is present but, in general, is defined as partiality in the cause of distinct national interests. This is misleading. While all the member states of the EC have democratic political systems, their governments are not always representative of the broad span of domestic interests within their countries. Inevitably governments respond preferentially to those sections of public opinion that help to conserve them in office, or to constituencies whose electoral affiliation may be courted by particular attitudes to EC proposals.

The original Monnet idea of a technocratic conspiracy served the Community well in its earlier years in the sense that it provided an alibi for accentuating the Community's role at the expense of member states. Gradually, however, its limitations have become apparent. It is inappropriate as a mode for resolving fundamental issues of politics and economics since it can only side-step them. National policy processes may and have camouflaged this. This is, however, beginning to change. Bargaining within member states over Community issues is becoming explicitly more political. It is less easily confined within a narrow section of the policy élites, though this still varies from country to country. But, increasingly, Community issues are being brought into other domestic controversies. This was illustrated by the difficulties of the West German government in implementing the Sixth Directive on Value Added Tax harmonization. A resolution was possible late in 1979 only after a political compromise had been reached as to whether the national territorial application of the legislation should include East Germany. Similarly, the issue of Mediterranean enlargement has raised problems for the French government as it responds to claims for more favourable treatment for farmers in the south-west. Community institutions have been slow to accommodate this kind of political bargaining, though both the European Council and the directly elected Parliament are beginning to show its reverberations.

The following table sets out the range of factors relevant to the determination of national policies towards the EC. *Capacity* and *resources* include the basic attributes of the political, administrative, and economic systems of the member states. *Domestic constraints* are the demands on governments and the limitations on their freedom of manoeuvre; they are not peculiar to EC issues, but are as relevant to national management of EC policy as to other areas of national policy. *Extra-national constraints* are the commitments and the developments that flow either directly from the EC systems or from the international system more generally. *Goals* and *strategy* include both the formal objectives of national policies towards the EC and the goals that emerge as a by-product of other pressures and demands. The table includes illustrative examples under each heading.

The main purpose of the table is to identify the range and complexity of factors that influence national policy towards the EC. Unless all three strands—political, administrative, and economic—are incorporated and interrelated, any analysis is likely to be incomplete and superficial. The table

FACTORS AFFECTING NATIONAL POLICIES

	POLITICAL	ADMINISTRATIVE	ECONOMIC
Capacity and Resources	Stability of regime Cohesion of government Domestic political leadership Public acceptance of EC Agreed procedures for conflict resolution Scope for autonomous national policies	Structure, status, & morale Availability of appropriate skills Multilateral experience Knowledge of other member states Mechanisms for policy management	Share of EC GNP Share of EC agriculture/trade/industry Rate of economic growth Availability of capital, labour, etc. Strength of currency Contributions to EC budget
Domestic Constraints	General political conflict Dissensus over EC Other domestic issues Lobbies on EC issues Parliamentary scrutiny Party considerations	Deployment of personnel Bureaucratic competition Relations between ministers & officials Compatibility of national and EC policies Problems of policy implementation	Rate of inflation Domestic claims on exchequer Domestic economic problems Roles of public & private bodies in economy Compatibility of domestic economy with EC
Extra-National Constraints	Other international commitments Alternative forums to EC Relations with EC partners EC influence on individual careers EC leverage on national politicians	Links with other administrations EC influence on national bargaining power EC influence on careers EC as source of new ideas	Economic interdependence with EC Economic links outside EC Balance of payments Pressure on currency Dependence on imports and exports Migrant labour Foreign investment
Goals and Strategy	Attitude to EC institutions Attitude to EC policy scope Sectoral objectives National priorities Other international objectives	EC as vehicle for seeking or preventing change Opportunities for coalition formation	Access to EC funds Resource transfers Increased economic opportunities Other international economic aims Protection of national economy

EC = European Community

provides a set of yardsticks, from which distinct national profiles can be empirically deduced. The congruence between national economic and political factors on the one hand and current Community policies on the other is very high in some cases—for example, the Netherlands and Ireland. The governments of such countries can readily adopt stances that favour further "integration" while at the same time they are confident that, by and large, increased EC activity is likely to coincide with their assessment of their national interests. At the other end of the spectrum is a dissonance between current Community policies and the economic and political interests sought by the United Kingdom. This makes government policy more circumspect and public attitudes more cautious. In between are the examples of France and Denmark, where there is congruence on some issues and conflict on others. This leads to the paradox that the governments of these two countries are among the Community's staunchest and most orthodox supporters on some issues, while they resist Community interference with equal vigour on issues where their domestic definitions of interest diverge sharply from the prevalent view of the Community as a collectivity. This demonstrates how closely progress in EC bargaining depends on the deep-rooted political and economic concerns of the member states.

The administrative or intra-governmental column represents the scope that the policy élites of the member states have for articulating national policies between the two levels—national and Community. National policy makers have the opportunity to leaven, mediate, and exploit as they interpret their own countries to the Community and their partners and as they interpret the latter back to their own domestic audiences. Some do this with more skill and panache than others, for reasons of history, confidence, and political status. Some are more permeable to Community influence than others. The record of EC agreements over the years demonstrates the differential abilities of member governments to achieve their own policy goals and to exercise leadership within the Community as a whole. A broad distinction can be drawn between those governments that have pursued active and innovative policies towards the EC and those that have adopted reactive and often defensive approaches. However, this distinction does not entirely coincide with the division between the congruent and the non-congruent. The examples of France and Germany illustrate this. The French government, the economic and political interests of which were not readily compatible with the obvious Community consensus, succeeded by an active and assertive policy in forging congruence out of a potential clash of interest. By contrast, German governments, whose material and political interests closely coincided with the central elements of EC consensus, have until recently preferred to ride with rather than shape positively the prevalent middle ground of the Community.

CONCLUSIONS

Two main conclusions flow from this analysis. First, the establishment and maintenance of a Community consensus depends on its congruence with the political and economic interests of its members. The achievement of congruence has become more difficult as the policy issues at stake have become more intractable. Two rounds of enlargement have complicated this further by introducing members some of whose interests do not easily coincide with the core of the compact originally struck among the Six. The possible emergence of a two-tier or à la carte Community will be a function of how far the Community collectively proves capable of aggregating diverse and sometimes conflicting political and economic interests within a band of common policies. Secondly, Community issues have become more controversial and have penetrated deeply into the member states, precisely because of their political and economic ramifications. Proposals for new Community policies or changes in current policies require not just the acceptance of member governments, but the active consent of both sectional groups and domestic public opinion more broadly. Since EC negotiations still depend primarily on bargaining among member governments, the shaping of public attitudes is still largely dependent on cues from individual governments to their own constituents. The scope for Community institutions to act directly on the politics of the member states remains limited, though the directly elected Parliament may change this.

What then are the implications for a broader evaluation of the character of the Community? The process at work bites more deeply into the political fabric of the member states than economic interdependence alone can explain. Forces are certainly at work that cut across national boundaries, yet the label "transnationalism" does not entirely do justice to them. The clustering of entrenched vested interests around the *acquis communautaire* is formidable. But in other areas, the forging of Community-wide coalitions has proved elusive, and indeed the manifestations of economic and political divergence suggest that complementarity, let alone compatibility, of material interests cannot be readily established. The Community framework does not yet rest on the bedrock of a sense of political community widespread enough in all the member states or different sections of popular opinion to sustain a progressive transfer of authority from the national to the Community level. Governments can and do retain a crucial function as filters between the two levels, though the Community process is pervasive enough for some of its influence to seep past and through the filters.

Both the theorist and the practitioner are thus left to puzzle out the implications of this rather untidy picture. Perhaps the closest we can come to characterizing the essence of the Community is to assert that it has become a highly politicized process that reflects and generates conflict over real and significant economic issues. Its capacity to resolve conflict varies from sector to sector depending on how far Community authority is established and on whether the separate interests of member states or economic groups can be aggregated. The most difficult question to resolve is whether the process is incremental. The continuum posited by the neo-functionalists of a slide from economic to political integration cannot be demonstrated. Yet the scope and activities of the Community are continually being extended, often in a fragmented way and rarely by great leaps forward. A major problem facing the Community is that the issues currently on its agenda are difficult and sensitive in terms of both domestic politics and economic policies. It has become fashionable to argue that the Community has reached a stage in its history where it must either take a quantum leap forward or fall back into a pale shadow of its former self. This dichotomy is too stark. Enough interests have probably already become vested in Community policies to hold together a significant measure of intensive collaboration. But as long as congruence cannot be established on the other major points at issue, both member governments and their constituents are likely to refrain from accepting significant extensions of political authority for the EC. This suggests a parallelism in the two tracks of economic and political integration, rather than that the one is a condition of the other.

NOTES

[1] See Carole Webb, "Variations on a Theoretical Theme," in *Policy Making in the European Communities*, edited by H. Wallace, W. Wallace, and C. Webb (London: John Wiley, 1977).

[2] See Ralf Dahrendorf, "A Third Europe?" 3rd Monnet Lecture (Florence: European University Institute, 1979); and Michael Hodges, "The Legacy of the Treaty of Rome: A Community of Equals," *World Today* 35 (June 1979): 232-40. For a different approach, see John Pinder, "Integrating Divergent Economies: The Extranational Method," *International Affairs* (October 1979):546-58.

[3] See, for example, C. Sasse *et al.*, *Decision Making in the European Communities* (New York: Praeger, 1977); V. Herman and R. van Schendelen, *The European Parliament and the National Parliaments* (Farnborough: Saxon House, 1979); and C. Hull and R.A.W. Rhodes, *Intergovernmental Relations in the European Community* (Farnborough: Saxon House, 1977).

[4] These include J. Rideau, *La France et les Communautés Européennes* (Paris: LGDJ, 1975); D. Coombes, *The British People: Their Voice in Europe* (Farnborough: Saxon House, 1977); and P. Vannicelli, *Italy, NATO and the European Community: The Interplay of Foreign Policy and Domestic Politics* (Cambridge, Mass.: Harvard University Center for International Affairs, 1974).

[5] For a summary see Webb, *op. cit.*, especially pp. 13-15.

[6] The French government's attitude to the judgement of the European Court of Justice on sheepmeat during autumn 1979 is an unusual example.

[7] See H. Wallace, W. Wallace, and C. Webb, eds., *Policy Making in the European Communities* (London: John Wiley, 1977), Chapters 3, 5, and 6 on economic, industrial, and regional policies respectively.

[8] See Michael Hodge, ed., *Economic Divergence in the European Community* (London: Allen and Unwin, forthcoming), and Loukas Tsoukalis, *The Politics and Economics of European Monetary Integration* (London: Allen and Unwin, 1977).

[9] See, for example, the change in the attitudes of French industrialists from strong opposition to the ECSC in 1950-51 to recognition of its benefits and support for further integration. F. Roy Willis, *France, Germany and the New Europe, 1945-1967*, 2d ed. (London: Oxford University Press, 1968), pp. 94-98 and 232-34.

[10] In some instances such as textiles, the defensiveness was collectivized through Community participation in the Multi-Fibre Agreement. But in many others, from shipbuilding to motor cars, the emphasis was on maintaining a position within a national context.

[11] This was foreshadowed in France in the late 1960s and emerged in Britain during the mid-1970s.

[12] This in large part explains the failure of the Community to reform the CAP, given its continuing importance for agricultural voters and those who identify with them and their relevance to coalition formation in some member states.

[13] For a fuller analysis see Helen Wallace, *Budgetary Politics: The Finances of the European Community* (London: Allen and Unwin, 1980).

[14] This is most evident in the central areas of economic policy, and illustrated by the difficulties of the EC in establishing industrial, regional, and energy policies. See Wallace *et al.*, *op. cit.*, Chapters 5, 6, and 7.

[15] Most evident so far in Britain, and on some issues in Denmark and France, but increasingly emerging in other member states as well.

[16] See William Wallace, ed., *Britain in Europe* (London: Heinemann, 1980).

Conclusion

The six chapters comprising the substance of this book shed considerable light upon the nature of regionalism, federalism, and supranationalism, and upon their manifestations in Western Europe and Canada. These concluding observations are drawn from the preceding chapters and from the two-day seminar discussion within the context of which the six papers were first presented. No attempt has been made to offer an accurate reproduction of the discussions that actually occurred. Rather, the editor has sought to identify themes and general conclusions that underscore the present analysis, and lessons that might inform future inquiries.

One of the most outstanding characteristics of both the papers and the discussions was revealed in the very different perspectives Canadians and Europeans brought to a consideration of federalism. Canadian scholars, undoubtedly reflecting the Canadian political system itself, approached questions of regionalism and supranationalism almost entirely in relation to federalism. For the Canadians, regionalism was invariably identified with provincialism (as in Raymond Breton's Chapter Four), and its strength seen in terms of the relative decentralization required of the Canadian federation in order to contain, accommodate, or encourage it as the individual might prefer. Precisely because centralization and decentralization were considered within the context of a domestic federal arrangement, the notion of supranationalism was alien to most Canadians. Continental integration is certainly one within the full range of conceptual options available for speculative inquiry, but as Denis Stairs points out in Chapter Five, it is not an option actively promoted by any significant academic or political group. Supranationalism is thus viewed by Canadians as continentalism, and the latter is easily and often transformed into American penetration, if not active imperialism.

In Canada, the tension between larger and smaller political units is thus a domestic issue and is invariably represented as a tension surrounding the appropriate strengths of the central and provincial governments within a federal arrangement (indeed, all but the most extreme of Quebec's *indépendantistes* accept the conclusion that the realistic political options open to that most nationalistic of Canada's regions all involve some form of association with the rest of Canada). It follows from this that Canadians have a good deal of difficulty coming to terms with the concept even of nationalism. To accord nationalistic attributes to the federal (or central) state is merely to join the federal-provincial tug of war on the side of the former. To bestow such attributes upon a province is to step outside the federal bounds, which define the limits of legitimate constitutional change. Political

127

debate among Canadians, reflected in this seminar discussion as well, starts and stops with the concept of federalism. What is debated is the most appropriate federal arrangement. And since the scope for federal arrangements is virtually unlimited (as Ronald Watts notes in Chapter One), the capacity for debates about federalism in Canada is probably inexhaustible.

By contrast, the federal state gave way to the nation-state as the essential point of reference for European scholars. Regionalism for the Europeans was, as Jacques Vandamme demonstrates in Chapter Three, a phenomenon occurring within nation-states. Similarly, Helen Wallace's Chapter Six provides eloquent testimony to the extent to which supranational (i.e., European) integration is perceived as a form of integration amongst continuing nation-states. Thus, Europeans tended to have difficulty with the concept of federalism somewhat comparable to Canadians' problems with nationalism. Europeans are quite familiar with federalism, of course, when it operates at the level of the nation-state. Indeed, the essence of Gordon Smith's conclusions in Chapter Two constitute an argument in favour of the adoption of federalism by additional states. On that point Europeans were every bit as capable as Canadians in arguing about the fine points of political decentralization and the need or the lack of need for strong central governments. European scholars seemed united, however, in dismissing the possibility that a continuing integration of Western Europe might eventually yield a supranational political community and thus a true European federation. European federation was often cited as a possibility—one colourful description referred to the possibility in terms of "creeping federalism"—but this was always conceived as a federation of nation-states. Europe as a federation of federations emerged as the logical if unmentioned product of this analysis.

Canadians and Europeans were in remarkable accord regarding the nature of regionalism. Jacques Vandamme's distinction between regionalization—the deliberate creation of regions for purposes of central policy—and true regionalism was seen as being of equal validity in Canada. Similarly, Europeans agreed with Raymond Breton that the identity of Canada's regions with the provinces of a federation gave to Canadian regionalism a powerful vehicle for the formulation and implementation of regional policies. It was precisely this identity of the region within a regional state that led several Europeans to promote the idea of federalism for such regionalized but constitutionally unitary states as Belgium and the United Kingdom.

Supranationalism, as already noted, created the greatest difficulty. The very concept of supranationalism is alien to the Canadian vocabulary, unless used pejoratively to describe American continentalist pressures. For Europeans, the concept was familiar enough, but it invariably evoked strong feelings when attempts were made to suggest the constitutional or institutional form it might take in Europe.

Europeans and Canadians shared the common conclusion that contemporary political life is witnessing an interesting and important tension between forces—largely economic—pressing for larger states, and forces—largely cultural—pressing for smaller states. Both were quick to see in federalism a structural arrangement potentially capable of containing this tension. Canadians, because they essentially dismissed the notion of supranationalism, were able to reduce the tension to the appropriate balance of federal and provincial powers and thus to treat federalism almost as part of the problem itself. Europeans, because they gave central place to the idea of the nation-state, were able to consider federalism as an appropriate response to both regionalism and supranationalism. Interestingly, the two federalisms could be very different, and the same person who argued for a highly centralized, if federalized nation-state was quite capable of insisting on the most decentralized, if federalized, European Community. And both could be argued as inherent in the nature of federalism.

In this, Canadians and Europeans undoubtedly reflected and were conditioned by the choices and the values emerging from their respective political experiences. It is not surprising, then, that they should approach the concepts of regionalism, federalism, and supranationalism from different perspectives. What is more important is that they should hold so much in common. Quite clearly Canadians and Europeans—at least those who participated in this seminar—are coming to a common understanding of regionalism. It is an understanding, moreover, whose association of regional expression with political instrumentalities contains important lessons for the future of regional and federal government in both places. This growing awareness and knowledge of regionalism—its origins, forms, and consequences—is perhaps the single most important achievement of this project.

Of almost equal importance is the realization of the different meanings, and values, that can be placed upon the concept of federalism in different contexts. But then, as Ronald Watts notes in Chapter One, ''federalism is a pragmatic, prudential technique whose continued applicability may depend upon further innovations in its institutional variables.'' Much can be learned from a comparative approach to Europe and Canada. A great deal more remains to be learned about regionalism, federalism, and supranationalism.

The POLICY STUDIES INSTITUTE (PSI) is a British independent policy research organisation concerned with issues relevant to economic and social policies and the working of political institutions.

PSI was formed in April 1978 through the merger of Political and Economic Planning (PEP), founded in 1931, and the Centre for Studies in Social Policy (CSSP), founded in 1972. It continues the tradition of both organisations to establish the facts by impartial empirical research and to relate the findings to practical policy making. The scope of the Institute's work has been extended by the recent establishment of a European Centre for Political Studies. PSI's work is financed by grants for specific studies made by trusts, foundations and public bodies, with substantial support from donations by industry and commerce, and by annual subscriptions.

The results of the studies are disseminated widely by means of frequent publications, articles and seminars.

Details of subscription rates and recent publications will be sent on request.

1-2 Castle Lane, London SW1E 6DR
Telephone: 01-825-7055

Studies in European Politics
This series provides brief and up-to-date analyses of European political issues, including developments in the European Community and in transnational political forces, and also major problems in particular European countries. The research is undertaken by the European Centre for Political Studies, established in 1978 at the Policy Studies Institute with the sponsorship of the European Cultural Foundation. The series is edited by the Head of the Centre, Dr. Roger Morgan.

Already published
1. The Future of the European Parliament   *David Coombes*
2. Towards Transnational Parties in the European Community   *Geoffrey & Pippa Pridham*
3. European Integration, Regional Devolution and National Parliaments   *D. Coombes, R. Hrbek, S. Schüttemeyer, L. Condorelli, W. Parsons*
4. Eurocommunism: the Foreign Policy Dimensions   *Carole Webb*
5. Europe Elects Its Parliament   *Geneviève Bibes, Henri Ménudier, Françoise de la Serre, Marie-Claude Smouts*

Of related interest
Westminster and Devolution   *Study of Parliament Group in association with PSI*

The Institute for Research on Public Policy
PUBLICATIONS AVAILABLE*
January 1981

BOOKS

Leroy O. Stone &
Claude Marceau

*Canadian Population Trends and Public Policy
Through the 1980s*. 1977 $4.00

Raymond Breton

*The Canadian Condition: A Guide to Research in
Public Policy*. 1977 $2.95

Raymond Breton

*Une orientation de la recherche politique dans le
contexte canadien*. 1978 $2.95

J.W. Rowley &
W.T. Stanbury, eds.

Competition Policy in Canada: Stage II, Bill C-13.
1978 $12.95

C.F. Smart &
W.T. Stanbury, eds.

Studies on Crisis Management. 1978 $9.95

W.T. Stanbury, ed.

Studies on Regulation in Canada. 1978 $9.95

Michael Hudson

*Canada in the New Monetary Order: Borrow?
Devalue? Restructure!* 1978 $6.95

W.A.W. Neilson &
J.C. MacPherson, eds.

*The Legislative Process in Canada: The Need for
Reform*. 1978 $12.95

David K. Foot, ed.

*Public Employment and Compensation in Canada:
Myths and Realities*. 1978 $10.95

W.E. Cundiff &
Mado Reid, eds.

*Issues in Canada/U.S. Transborder Computer Data
Flows*. 1979 $6.50

G.B. Reschenthaler &
B. Roberts, eds.

Perspectives on Canadian Airline Regulation. 1979
$13.50

P.K. Gorecki &
W.T. Stanbury, eds.

*Perspectives on the Royal Commission on
Corporate Concentration*. 1979 $15.95

David K. Foot

Public Employment in Canada: Statistical Series.
1979 $15.00

---

* Order Address: The Institute for Research on Public Policy
P.O. Box 9300, Station A
TORONTO, Ontario
M5W 2C7

133

Meyer W. Bucovetsky, ed.	*Studies on Public Employment and Compensation in Canada.* 1979 $14.95
Richard French & André Béliveau	*The RCMP and the Management of National Security.* 1979 $6.95
Richard French & André Béliveau	*La GRC et la gestion de la sécurité nationale.* 1979 $6.95
Leroy O. Stone & Michael J. MacLean	*Future Income Prospects for Canada's Senior Citizens.* 1979 $7.95
Douglas G. Hartle	*Public Policy Decision Making and Regulation.* 1979 $12.95
Richard Bird (in collaboration with Bucovetsky & Foot)	*The Growth of Public Employment in Canada.* 1979 $12.95
G. Bruce Doern & Allan M. Maslove, eds.	*The Public Evaluation of Government Spending.* 1979 $10.95
Richard Price, ed.	*The Spirit of the Alberta Indian Treaties.* 1979 $8.95
Peter N. Nemetz, ed.	*Energy Policy: The Global Challenge.* 1979 $16.95
Richard J. Schultz	*Federalism and the Regulatory Process.* 1979 $1.50
Richard J. Schultz	*Le fédéralisme et le processus de réglementation.* 1979 $1.50
Lionel D. Feldman & Katherine A. Graham	*Bargaining for Cities. Municipalities and Intergovernmental Relations: An Assessment.* 1979 $10.95
Elliot J. Feldman & Neil Nevitte, eds.	*The Future of North America: Canada, the United States, and Quebec Nationalism.* 1979 $7.95
Maximo Halty-Carrere	*Technological Development Strategies for Developing Countries.* 1979 $12.95
G.B. Reschenthaler	*Occupational Health and Safety in Canada: The Economics and Three Case Studies.* 1979 $5.00
David R. Protheroe	*Imports and Politics: Trade Decision-Making in Canada, 1968–1979.* 1980 $8.95

G. Bruce Doern	*Government Intervention in the Canadian Nuclear Industry.* 1980 $8.95
G. Bruce Doern & R.W. Morrison, eds.	*Canadian Nuclear Policies.* 1980 $14.95
W.T. Stanbury, ed.	*Government Regulation: Scope, Growth, Process.* 1980 $10.95
Yoshi Tsurumi with Rebecca R. Tsurumi	*Sogoshosha: Engines of Export-Based Growth.* 1980 $8.95
Allan M. Maslove & Gene Swimmer	*Wage Controls in Canada, 1975−78: A Study in Public Decision Making.* 1980 $11.95
T. Gregory Kane	*Consumers and the Regulators: Intervention in the Federal Regulatory Process.* 1980 $10.95
Albert Breton & Anthony Scott	*The Design of Federations.* 1980 $6.95
A.R. Bailey & D.G. Hull	*The Way Out: A More Revenue-Dependent Public Sector and How It Might Revitalize the Process of Governing.* 1980 $6.95
Réjean Lachapelle & Jacques Henripin	*La situation démolinguistique au Canada: évolution passée et prospective.* 1980 $24.95
Raymond Breton, Jeffrey G. Reitz & Victor F. Valentine	*Cultural Boundaries and the Cohesion of Canada.* 1980 $18.95
David R. Harvey	*Christmas Turkey or Prairie Vulture? An Economic Analysis of the Crow's Nest Pass Grain Rates.* 1980 $10.95
Stuart McFadyen, Colin Hoskins & David Gillen	*Canadian Broadcasting: Market Structure and Economic Performance.* 1980 $15.95
Richard M. Bird	*Taxing Corporations.* 1980 $6.95
Albert Breton & Raymond Breton	*Why Disunity? An Analysis of Linguistic and Regional Cleavages in Canada.* 1980 $6.95
Leroy O. Stone & Susan Fletcher	*A Profile of Canada's Older Population.* 1980 $7.95

Peter N. Nemetz, ed.

Resource Policy: International Perspectives.
1980 $18.95

Keith A.J. Hay, ed.

Canadian Perspectives on Economic Relations with Japan. 1980 $18.95

Raymond Breton and
Gail Grant

La langue de travail au Québec: synthèse de la recherche sur la rencontre de deux langues.
1981 $10.95

Diane Vanasse

L'évolution de la population scolaire du Québec.
1981 $

Raymond Breton,
Jeffrey G. Reitz and
Victor F. Valentine

Les frontières culturelles et la cohésion du Canada.
1981 $18.95

David M. Cameron, ed.

Regionalism and Supranationalism: Challenges and Alternatives to the Nation-State in Canada and Europe. 1981 $9.95

Peter Aucoin, ed.

The Politics and Management of Restraint in Government. 1981 $17.95

OCCASIONAL PAPERS

W.E. Cundiff
(No. 1)

Nodule Shock? Seabed Mining and the Future of the Canadian Nickel Industry. 1978 $3.00

IRPP/Brookings
(No. 2)

Conference on Canadian-U.S. Economic Relations.
1978 $3.00

Robert A. Russel
(No. 3)

The Electronic Briefcase: The Office of the Future.
1978 $3.00

C.C. Gotlieb
(No. 4)

Computers in the Home: What They Can Do for Us—And to Us. 1978 $3.00

Raymond Breton &
Gail Grant Akian
(No. 5)

Urban Institutions and People of Indian Ancestry.
1978 $3.00

K.A. Hay
(No. 6)

Friends or Acquaintances? Canada as a Resource Supplier to the Japanese Economy. 1979 $3.00

T. Atkinson
(No. 7)

Trends in Life Satisfaction. 1979 $3.00

M. McLean
(No. 8)

The Impact of the Microelectronics Industry on the Structure of the Canadian Economy. 1979 $3.00

Fred Thompson &
W.T. Stanbury
(No. 9)

The Political Economy of Interest Groups in the Legislative Process in Canada. 1979 $3.00

Gordon B. Thompson
(No. 10)

Memo from Mercury: Information Technology **Is** *Different*. 1979 $3.00

Pierre Sormany
(No. 11)

Les micro-esclaves: vers une bio-industrie canadienne. 1979 $3.00

K. Hartley, P.N. Nemetz,
S. Schwartz, D. Uyeno,
I. Vertinsky & J. Young
(No. 12)

Energy R & D Decision Making for Canada. 1979 $3.00

David Hoffman &
Zavis P. Zeman, eds.
(No. 13)

The Dynamics of the Technological Leadership of the World. 1980 $3.00

Russell Wilkins

(No. 13*a*)

Health Status in Canada, 1926–1976. 1980 $3.00

Russell Wilkins
(No. 13*b*)

L'état de santé au Canada, 1926–1976. 1980 $3.00

P. Pergler
(No. 14)

The Automated Citizen: Social and Political Impact of Interactive Broadcasting. 1980 $4.95

Zavis P. Zeman
(No. 15)

Men with the Yen. 1980 $5.95

Donald G. Cartwright
(No. 16)

Official-Language Populations in Canada: Patterns and Contacts. 1980 $4.95

REPORT
Dhiru Patel

Dealing With Interracial Conflict: Policy Alternatives. 1980 $5.95

WORKING PAPERS (No Charge)**
W.E. Cundiff
(No. 1)

Issues in Canada/U.S. Transborder Computer Data Flows. 1978 (Out of print; in IRPP book of same title.)

John Cornwall   *Industrial Investment and Canadian Economic*
(No. 2)   *Growth: Some Scenarios for the Eighties.* 1978

Russell Wilkins   *L'espérance de vie par quartier à Montréal, 1976:*
(No. 3)   *un indicateur social pour la planification.* 1979

F.J. Fletcher &   *Canadian Attitude Trends, 1960—1978.* 1979
R.J. Drummond
(No. 4)

** Order Working Papers from
   The Institute for Research on Public Policy
   P.O. Box 3670
   Halifax South
   Halifax, Nova Scotia
   B3J 3K6